T0305286

COPY THIS BOOK!

COPY THIS BOOK!

*What Data Tells Us about Copyright
and the Public Good*

Paul J. Heald

STANFORD UNIVERSITY PRESS
Stanford, California

STANFORD UNIVERSITY PRESS
Stanford, California

Printed in the United States of America on acid-free, archival-quality paper

Library of Congress Cataloging-in-Publication Data
Names: Heald, Paul J., 1959– author.
Title: Copy this book! : what data tells us about copyright and the public good /
    Paul Heald.
Description: Stanford, California : Stanford University Press, 2020. | Includes index. |
    Includes bibliographical references and index
Identifiers: LCCN 2020025584 (print) | LCCN 2020025585 (ebook) |
    ISBN 9781503613959 (cloth) | ISBN 9781503614307 (paperback) |
    ISBN 9781503614314 (epub)
Subjects: LCSH: Copyright—United States.
Classification: LCC KF2994 .H373 2020 (print) | LCC KF2994 (ebook) |
    DDC 346.7304/82—dc23
LC record available at https://lccn.loc.gov/2020025584
LC ebook record available at https://lccn.loc.gov/2020025585

Book design: Kevin Barrett Kane

Typeset at Stanford University Press in 10/15 Minion Pro

For Pandy, Minis, Eddie, Love, Maddie,
Wilbur, Maizey, and Ernie

CONTENTS

PREFACE

I love copyright law. As a writer, I enjoy exclusive rights granted to me by Congress and am motivated by the profit that copyright seeks to guarantee me. I am a direct beneficiary of the system that I criticize.

I like water, too . . . but I don't want to drown in it.

ACKNOWLEDGMENTS

This book was written primarily during my time as a fellow at the Stellenbosch Institute for Advanced Study (STIAS), Wallenberg Research Centre at Stellenbosch University, Stellenbosch 7600, South Africa. I also received support during my sabbatical from the wonderful Professor Richard Watt and the University of Canterbury, Christchurch, New Zealand, during my stay there as an Erskine Fellow. To the extent that the book draws on previously published work, I'd like to thank the University of Georgia College of Law and the University of Illinois for generous research support. The audiobook study mentioned briefly in chapter 4 was supported by a small grant from Google. At the risk of forgetting someone, I'd like to thank my research assistants over the years, who include Kenny Barr, Meghan Blakely, Jessica Bregant, Sam Enkhbat, Tedra Hobson, Kacy King, Anne Lewis, Frank Madden, Laura Meli, Marissa Meli, Carolina van Mousel, Christian Perrin, Sivram Prasad, Rossana Rodriguez, Carlos Ruiz, Tyler Slack, Stephanie Steele, Jarrett Szczesny, Mark Tan, Andrea Wallace, Xiaoren Wang, Liz Wheeler, Xiaoren Xi, Dacheng Xie, and Xi Zhao. Let me specially thank Professor Martin Kretschmer and the folks at CREATe at the University of Glasgow, who have been wonderfully supportive of my copyright endeavors, and Peter Riva, my tireless and patient literary agent. Finally, any reader of the book will guess that I'm either a musician or married to one (it's the latter)—I would be nowhere without Jill Crandall, a fabulous musician and an even better wife and partner. Thank you all!

A BRIEF NOTE ON COPYRIGHT LAW
AND THE PURPOSE OF THIS BOOK

In a nutshell, anything you write on paper or at a computer (or compose or record or sketch or paint or photograph) is protected by copyright law, which means that you can sue someone who unfairly copies from your work. The Constitution authorizes Congress to provide this protection, and during the first session (March 4, 1789, to March 4, 1791) of the newly formed Congress, the legislature granted book authors and map makers (but only book authors and map makers) a 14-year term of copyright for their writings.[1]

The founders' main theory was that without adequate incentives, creative people would not produce the optimal amount of new stuff. Without protection, artists and authors would get ripped off by copyists and lose heart (and dollars). A corollary of their incentive theory provides that when copyright expires, the protected work shifts into the public domain for us to enjoy for free and—just as important—for the next generation of artists to use as the basis for yet more creation. That's the copyright bargain baked into the Constitution, which states in article 1, section 1, clause 8, that Congress can enact copyright laws only "to promote the progress of Science [meaning "knowledge" at the time it was written]."

This book uses data and empirical methods to ask big questions about copyright. What sort of copyright laws best promote public welfare? Why shouldn't all copying be prohibited? What is the best way to both protect authors and promote creativity?

Justices O'Connor and Brennan provided an important backdrop to these questions by explaining that in the US, the primary purpose of copyright is to increase public welfare, not to make authors rich: "It may seem unfair that much of the fruit of the compiler's labor may be used by others without compensation.

[However], this is not 'some unforeseen byproduct of a statutory scheme.' It is, rather, 'the essence of copyright,' and a constitutional requirement. The primary objective of copyright is not to reward the labor of authors, but 'to promote the Progress of Science and useful Arts.'"[2]

Nowadays, authors, musicians, dramatists, choreographers, painters, sculptors, architects, and photographers all have strong protection that extends until 70 years after their deaths.[3] Since the founding of our country, both the length and breadth of copyright protection has expanded, with more extensive protection proposed every year (see table 0.1).

Copyright law is not so complicated that the layperson is unable to determine what sort of legal protection is sensible and what sort is merely the result of industry capture of Congress. The goal of this book is to tell the story of copyright through empirical research (illustrated with interesting case studies of familiar works) and thereby to provide the reader with the tools for judging the wisdom of past and future copyright legislation.

The introduction to this book starts with one of the most surprising stories about copyright—how it diminishes the availability of important books to the public. Subsequent chapters identify other consumer welfare problems caused by overprotection of copyright: orphan photographs with unfindable owners (chapter 1); ambiguous infringement rules that drive musicians crazy (chapter 2); and ludicrous—yet dangerous—claims publishers make over public domain works (chapter 6). Although too much copyright clearly causes problems, the

TABLE 0.1. Dates When Congress First Enacted Copyright Protection.

1. Literary works (books, maps, and charts) (1790)

2. Musical works, including any accompanying words (1831)

3. Dramatic works, including any accompanying music (1856)

4. Pantomimes and choreographic works (1976)

5. Pictorial, graphic, and sculptural works (1865; 1871)

6. Motion pictures and other audiovisual works (1912)

7. Sound recordings (1971)

8. Architectural works (1990)

Source: 17 U.S.C. § 106 (2018).

empirical story is not all sadness. Rights reversion statutes bring books back into print (chapter 3), and the study of parody (including porn parodies!) reveals a healthy resilience in the copyright system (chapters 4 and 5). The book then fills out the complex empirical story of how creativity is fostered in the US by explaining how the music industry thrived despite the infringement onslaught of peer-to-peer file sharing (chapter 8); how the lack of legal protection for public domain photographs created massive value on Wikipedia (chapter 7); and how the lack of legal protection for public domain music influenced the film industry (chapter 10).

The book ends with the story of the author's personal involvement in a Don Quixote–style attempt to convince the Supreme Court that the Sonny Bono Copyright Term Extension Act is unconstitutional and offers a rather implausible conspiracy theory that links copyright law to Second Amendment rights.

In between the entertaining anecdotes, the overall goal of the book should be easy to discern. A data-driven view of copyright should convince the reader to exclaim at least once, "Boy, that part of copyright law is total nonsense!"

COPY THIS BOOK!

DISAPPEARING BOOKS AND DEAD RATS AT THE TRANS-PACIFIC PARTNERSHIP

"The most alarming literary news in years is the enormous
success of James Gould Cozzens' *By Love Possessed.*"
—DWIGHT MACDONALD, Commentary (January 1, 1958)[1]

The Case of the Disappearing Books

One of the greatest literary controversies of the twentieth century revolved
around the worthiness of the book that knocked *Peyton Place*—once the bestselling novel of all time—off the top of the *New York Times* fiction list. James
Gould Cozzens's *By Love Possessed*, in a series of disturbing flashbacks, spins
the tepid-yet-lurid tale of a middle-aged lawyer prompted by sudden events to
contemplate his life. The book won the William Dean Howells medal in 1960
for the best work of fiction published in the prior five years and was made into
a movie in 1961 by John Sturges (*The Magnificent Seven*; *The Great Escape*).
After the novel had been on the bestseller list for 34 weeks, *Time* magazine put
Cozzens on its cover and declared his book "the best American novel in years."

The ceaseless praise for the novel became too much for Dwight Macdonald, a prominent literary critic. In one of the most damning—and effective—-
-reviews in history, Macdonald canvassed the existing praise for Cozzens's work
and wrote, "This sincere enthusiasm for mediocre work is more damaging to
literary standards than any amount of cynical ballyhoo." He pronounced the
novel's hero "a prig" and found Cozzens to be "guilty of the unforgiveable nov-
elistic sin: he is unaware of the real nature of his characters." So vicious was his

review that one Cozzens commentator declared Macdonald's essay "a famous document in the history of higher critical demolition," an attack that rendered Cozzens "infamous."[2]

I hesitate to enter the debate over the quality of *By Love Possessed* (although one look at the movie trailer might push you in Macdonald's direction[3]); instead, I offer an observation: although *By Love Possessed* is undoubtedly one of the most prominent works of fiction in the last half of the twentieth century, you cannot go to Amazon.com (or anyplace else) and buy a new copy. It's been out of print for years.

How can one of the bestselling and most controversial novels of the century not be available from Amazon Prime?

Unfortunately, the unavailability of a new paperback, hardback, or Kindle of *By Love Possessed* is hardly unusual. Numerous bestsellers, many of which I remember lining my parent's bookshelves, like *The Tontine* by Thomas Costain and Robert Ruark's *Something of Value*, have long since gone out of print. Other missing bestsellers from the same era include *The War Lover* by John Hersey (author of *Hiroshima*, *The Wall*, and *A Bell for Adano*); *Seven Days in May* by Fletcher Knebel (you might remember the 1964 movie of the same title starring Burt Lancaster and Kirk Douglas); *Kalki* by Gore Vidal (a finalist for the 1978 Nebula Award); *An Indecent Obsession* by Colleen McCullough (author of *The Thornbirds*); and other bestsellers by hugely popular authors like Taylor Caldwell, A. J. Cronin (whose books have been made into 19 movies!), Paul Erdman, Irving Stone, and Morris West.

The story gets much worse when we look at the availability of new editions of books on Amazon. Figure I.1 shows a random sample of more than 2,300 new books for sale by Amazon in 2012; pay attention to the initial publication date for each book.[4] The bar graph shows the books grouped by the decade in which they were first published.

Not surprisingly, Amazon sells quite a few new books from the decade of 2000 to 2010, more than 10 percent of the sample. More striking is how few titles are still in print from the 1930s to the 1980s, as well as how many titles are currently in print from decades prior to 1920.

Why are there so many more editions of books from the 1880s and 1890s in print than from the 1980s and 1990s? The answer is fairly simple: copyright law.

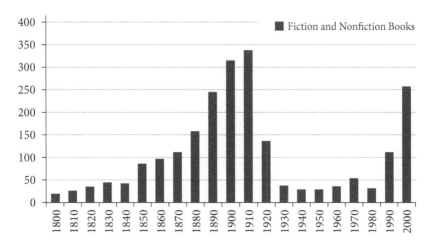

FIGURE I.1.   New Editions from Amazon by Original Decade of a Title's Publication, 1800–2000. Source: Data from Paul J. Heald, "How Copyright Keeps Works Disappeared," *Journal of Empirical Legal Studies* 18 (2014): 839.

In the US, at the time the sample was taken, all books published before 1923 were in the public domain, free for any publisher to print (or make into an ebook or audiobook) and sell. The books on the right side of the graph are still eligible for copyright protection, so when they go out of print, only the copyright owner (usually) has the right to bring them back for us.

So, the graph brings two phenomena to light. First, the big spike on the left side of the graph represents a group of publishers eager to put out new editions of most public domain books. Second, the plummeting line on the right side of the graph shows that copyright owners are disinterested in making new copies of older books available to us, even bestsellers.

Now, we can refine the data analysis in the graph to reflect the number of different *titles* available on Amazon (as opposed to the number of new *editions* of a book). Consider that Amazon currently offers more than 600 different new editions of John Milton's classic *Paradise Lost*, a work first published in 1667 and thus long in the public domain. When you take a random sample of new *editions* of books on Amazon, you will catch a disproportionate number of pre-1923 *titles* because multiple publishers can legally offer each title. In fact, public domain books typically have three times as many new editions as copyrighted

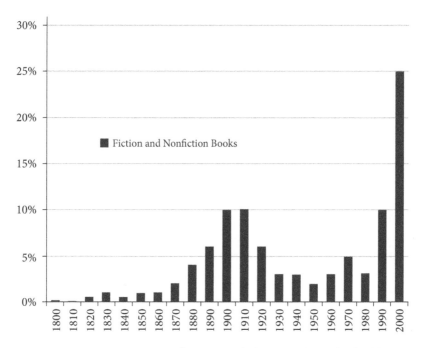

FIGURE I.2.   Estimate Percentage of Amazon Titles by Original Decade of Publication, 1800–2000. Source: Data from Heald, "How Copyright Keeps Works Disappeared," 841.

books (which typically have just two editions: hardcover and paperback). So, to show more accurately the effect of copyright on the distribution of titles, we need to adjust the graph to account for the difference in the average number of editions (see fig. I.2).

This picture looks a little less distorted until we remember how many fewer books were published in the late nineteenth and early twentieth centuries. In those decades, book markets were much smaller: there were fewer people, and a smaller percentage of the population was literate. Producing books using manual typesetting was also much more time-consuming. So, it's no surprise that only 105,000 books were registered for copyrights during the 1880s, whereas more than 1.4 million were registered during the 1980s. Fourteen times[5] as many books were published in the 1980s than the 1880s!

In other words, the distortion caused by copyright reflected in figure I.2 should be amplified to show that a random sample of Amazon titles should contain many times more books from the latter part of the twentieth century because so many more titles were printed then. If we use the number of copyright registrations per decade as a proxy for the number of books published (data that do not exist), we can paint the most accurate picture of the imbalance caused by copyright (see fig. I.3).

Given that as books age they naturally become less popular, we would expect the graph to show exactly the opposite. We would expect that most books in print would be from 2000 to 2010, followed by slightly fewer from the 1990s, fewer still from the 1980s, and gradually declining to the 1870s in a nice gradual downward line.

Instead, copyright keeps the more recent books out of print, distorting the natural decay of availability that we would expect to see. We end up with a disproportionate percentage of old books available to us, due to copyright's distorting effect.

So, why have copyright at all? If copyright so warps the market for new books, why should we accept the disappearance of millions of titles from the market?

The sensible standard argument is that without the protection provided by copyright, many authors would not produce works in the first place. Surely, we need copyright some of the time to stimulate creativity. I've published three novels, and without the ability to recoup my investment via the exclusive right to publish them, I would not have written them. Did I, however, need legal assurance

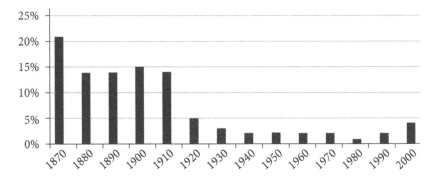

FIGURE I.3. Percentage of Amazon Titles Adjusted for Differential Publication Rates: By Original Decade of Publication, 1870–2000. Source: Data from Heald, "How Copyright Keeps Works Disappeared," 841.

that my exclusive rights would last my whole life plus 70 years? Intuitively, this seems longer than necessary, unless for paternalistic reasons Congress wants to make sure my great-grandchildren get royalties from my books.

Well, I love my progeny, but they need to go out and earn their own money. And I'm not alone in being snarky about the grandkids. Mark Twain approved of copyright term extension to 56 years in the 1909 Copyright Act, saying it "would take care of my daughters, and after that I am not particular."[6]

A much shorter term of protection should be more than enough to stimulate authors to write. Personal anecdotes, however, may not be convincing. Consider instead the seven Nobel Prize–winning economists who filed a brief with the Supreme Court stating that lengthening the term of copyright by 20 years—from life-of-the-author-plus-50 to life-of-the-author-plus-70—would provide "no significant contribution to an author's incentive to create."[7] Duh.

The Nobel Prize winners chimed in during the debate over the incentive effects of the 1998 extension of the copyright term to future works. It should be even easier to see that protecting existing works by dead authors cannot be plausibly justified under an incentive-to-create rationale. Clearly, in 1998, Ernest Hemingway did not need an incentive to write *The Sun Also Rises* (1926). Nonetheless, in 1998 Congress also extended the term of protection of all existing works (including Hemingway's) then under copyright for 20 years. The new protection prevented many famous older works from entering the public domain. In other words, the copyright in a work from 1925 that would have expired in 2000 was extended to the year 2020. Works from 1935 extended to 2030. Works from 1975 to 2070, and so on.

The extension helps explain why there are so few titles for sale on the right side of the graph in figures I.1, I.2, and I.3. The public domain was frozen for 20 years.

Despite the fact that *existing* books needed no incentive to be created, an alternative argument was offered to justify the 1998 retroactive term extension—an argument that sounded potentially plausible. Maybe publishers needed a longer term as an incentive to keep books in print. Maybe, in the absence of an extended property right, publishers would hesitate to make these works available to us.

The "increased availability" argument was my motivation for taking the random sample from Amazon.com, and you see what story it tells. Long copyright terms mean *decreased* availability for books.

So, data have settled the debate over the wisdom of copyright extensions for existing works, right? No plausible incentive-to-create argument or plausible incentive-to-make-available argument can be made. In fact, we see a mammoth decrease in distribution (and presumably in public welfare) due to term extension. It seems like a no-brainer that the US would stop advocating copyright term extensions. But ...

The Dead Rat in the Trans-Pacific Partnership

The US government spent a good part of the 2010s trying to convince Japan, Australia, New Zealand, Malaysia, Canada, Mexico, Chile, Peru, and several other Pacific Rim countries to enter into a new multilateral trade agreement, the Trans-Pacific Partnership (TPP).[8] The Trump administration has since withdrawn the US from participation,[9] but the US role in negotiating the copyright provisions of the agreement sheds much-needed light on who dictates US copyright policy. (Hint: It's not Nobel Prize–winning economists.)

US negotiators insisted that, to obtain access to the lucrative US market for manufactured and agricultural goods, all signatories to the TPP had to agree to extend the term of copyright protection 20 years for both existing works and future works. One can see why the US would push other nations to lengthen their terms of protection. We are a net exporter of copyrighted goods (think Hollywood and hip-hop), so earning an extra 20 years of foreign royalties should have a positive effect on the US economy.

However, the gains in foreign royalties are dwarfed by the cost of extended copyright protection within our own borders. Copyright makes royalties flow to American publishers, but American consumers have to pay too. Not surprisingly, goods protected by copyright are more expensive than royalty-free goods.[10] Are American consumers happy to pay higher prices because foreign consumers also have to pay the same premium?

The response of potential US trading partners in the Pacific Rim was negative. After all, they knew about figures I.1, I.2, and I.3.[11] Those countries could see the downside of extension: 20 years of increased prices and diminished accessibility. They objected to the extension provisions in the proposed TPP. Why should we, the foreign negotiators asked, make the same mistake the US made in 1998?

I recently heard an Australian economist offer a response: Australia needed to concede to the US demands and extend its copyright term to take advantage of the prior US extension that would help Aussie authors make more money in the US.

But this reciprocity argument is illusory: the US doesn't discriminate against foreign authors when it comes to protecting their works in the US. In other words, the US already gives Aussie and Kiwi and Japanese authors a full life-of-the-author-plus-70, despite the shorter copyright term in Australian, New Zealand, and Japanese law! Not hearing a legitimate public interest argument made in the TPP negotiations, commentators around the Pacific Rim concluded that they were being offered a "dead rat" to eat by the US.[12]

Potential members of the TPP also concluded that eating the rat was necessary to obtain access to the US market for other sorts of goods: "If copyright changes are the dead rat we have to eat with our otherwise-tasty Trans-Pacific Partnership meal, it is worth knowing a bit more about that rat."[13]

And what happened when the US withdrew from the treaty negotiations? The vermin was tossed in the garbage, and the US copyright proposals disappeared from the text of the agreement.

CHAPTER ONE

PHOTOGRAPHIC ORPHANS AND FRUSTRATED ADOPTIONS

ONE PROBLEM WITH LONG COPYRIGHT TERMS is that they leave the provenance of many works in serious doubt. The author of a work is the original copyright owner; however, identifying that author and tracing decades-old transfers is not always possible. A work without a clear owner is often called an orphan work. Consider the iconic 1932 photograph *Lunch atop a Skyscraper*[1] (fig. 1.1). Determining the copyright owner of a photo, or whether it is protected by copyright at all, turns out to be devilishly difficult. Even a copyright lawyer who camps in the copyright office and who purchases computer access to hundreds of private databases cannot tell for certain who owns the copyright in this picture.

Shockingly, Getty Images is happy to charge consumers more than $2,100 to use the image "in an editorial-style article (any placement—print or electronic) intended to indirectly promote a product or service."[2] Curiously, Getty does not claim to own the copyright. It will charge you less to make a poster.

Given the high price of a Getty license, those seeking to use the image are understandably interested in determining whether the image might be in the public domain and therefore free for anyone to use for any purpose.

This uncertain state of affairs seems odd because someone interested in finding the owner of a house, a vacant lot, or an automobile need only consult a registry of

FIGURE 1.1. *Lunch atop a Skyscraper*, Charles Ebbets, *New York Herald Tribune*, October 2, 1932. Source: Wikimedia Commons.

owners managed by the state or local government. Unfortunately, copyrights are "personal property," like rings and baseballs, and ownership of most personal property is not formally registered anywhere. Think about your jewelry or eyeglasses. There is no handy register to consult regarding whether you are the actual owner of your new Tiffany necklace or whether you borrowed it from a friend. Nonetheless, with most personal property, possession serves as an accurate substitute for a public register. In fact, the notice-serving function of possession is the real origin of the phrase "possession is nine-tenths of the law," because if you're wearing something or keeping it in your house or car, then you are most likely the owner.

The problem with copyright ownership becomes quickly apparent—it is a type of personal property that is intangible and invisible. Although you might possess a physical copy of a book or CD or DVD, that fact provides no clue as to whether you own the copyright in the underlying story or song or movie.

So, one would expect the US government to maintain an effective public registry of copyrights, whereby the interested public could check on their rights to use a work.

It doesn't, really.

Since 1976, copyright registration has been optional and, before that, registration was necessary only for those wanting to renew their copyrights 28 years after publication. In fact, our treaty obligations under the Berne Convention generally prohibit the US from requiring owners to register.[3] Even the more robust pre-1976 system was hardly a guarantee of clarity, especially for photographic works.

Let me relate, through gritted teeth, why we can make only an educated guess as to who, if anyone, owns the copyright in this wonderful picture of men lunching atop a skyscraper. Unfortunately, the story is representative of most photographic copyrights that the public might try to source.

Let's start with the photographer. For decades, Lewis Hine (1874–1940), a sociologist famous for his depiction of child labor across the US, was credited as having taken the picture.[4] Hamilton Wright, a documentary and promotional filmmaker, was also credited at one time.[5] But in 2003, Corbis, an image licensing company later absorbed by Getty Images, formally credited Charles C. Ebbets (1905–78).[6] Ebbets was the official photographer for legendary boxer Jack Dempsey as well as the chief photographer for the City of Miami for almost 20 years. Shortly after the photo was taken, he moved to Florida, where he gained international acclaim as an intimate chronicler of life among the Seminole Indians.[7]

Most relevantly, he also worked in New York as photographic director for the Rockefeller Center during its construction in 1932. His daughter, Tami Ebbets Hahn, found among her father's possessions a glass plate showing him on the beam in the photograph, along with other pictures of ironworkers likely to have been taken the same day.[8] She also has invoices billing Rockefeller Center for photos he took.

Having seen documentation held by Ebbets's daughter, I am satisfied that Ebbets took the picture; yet, I doubt that his estate can establish its ownership of the copyright.

Authorship and Ownership Are Not the Same Thing

The issue of who owns the photograph's copyright is governed by the 1909 Copyright Act, which was in force when the picture was taken. Under that Act, employers (and those resembling employers) were deemed to own the copyrights of works created at their "instance and expense." In the easiest case, works created by formal salaried employees were clearly owned by the employer. Works created by more independent contractors created difficulties for courts asked to determine ownership.

One of the most famous illustrations of the old 1909 Copyright Act rule involved the estate of Jack Kirby, the co-creator of Spiderman, Captain America, the Hulk, Thor, and other Marvel superheroes. According to the US Court of Appeals for the Second Circuit, Kirby was a freelancer who was "not paid a fixed wage or salary." Moreover, he "did not receive benefits," he "set his own hours and worked from his home," and his compensation was paid "at a per-page rate." Arguing that Kirby's work was not made-for-hire, his estate claimed an interest in the multibillion-dollar portfolio of characters that he created.[9] Given the court's description, Kirby hardly seemed like an employee of Marvel.

The test for pre-1978 works, however, focuses not on the formality of employment but on whether the work was created at the "instance and expense" of someone else.

The entire claim of the Kirby estate turned on how his relationship with Marvel should be characterized, and the Second Circuit upheld the trial court's finding that Kirby's work was made at the "instance and expense" of Marvel and therefore the copyright in his drawings had always belonged to Marvel. Luckily for Kirby's heirs, the case generated such bad publicity for Marvel that it eventually settled with the family.[10]

So, *Marvel Characters, Inc., v. Kirby* presents a stumbling block for Ebbets's claim *if* the photo was taken at the "instance and expense" of the Rockefeller Center. Ebbets was a freelancer who sold photos to multiple clients, including various newspapers.[11] If he was constantly taking photos at his own expense, bearing the risk that they would go unpurchased, then his estate may well be able to argue the *Kirby* case is not good precedent. Either way, the inquiry is fact-heavy and would require a hard look at Ebbets's relationship with the Rockefeller Center.

The second problem for Ebbets's estate is much more serious.

The photo was first published in the *New York Herald Tribune* on October 2, 1932, without a copyright notice and without disclosure of the photographer's identity. Under the 1909 Copyright Act, [publication of a photo (or any kind of work) without "adequate notice" (including proper attribution) immediately put the work irretrievably into the public domain.

We might be tempted, therefore, to conclude that the work is clearly in the public domain. Unfortunately for lovers of clarity, the plot thickens once again. Because so many newspapers and periodicals failed to protect contributing photographers by affixing proper copyright notices to the photographs they published, judges invented a legal fiction to prevent photographic contributions from falling into the public domain.[12] Most courts found that the general copyright notice placed at the beginning of a newspaper or magazine, claiming copyright for the collective work as a whole, provided adequate notice for all the photos contained therein.[13] This sleight of hand saved millions of photos from falling instantly into the public domain upon publication, but it created a secondary issue. The copyright notice at the beginning of the newspaper typically claimed rights in favor of the newspaper, *not* the photographers.

Nonetheless, the copyright notice placed by the *New York Herald Tribune* at the front of the Sunday, October 2, 1932, issue almost certainly prevented Ebbets's famous photo from falling into the public domain upon its publication.

The 1909 Act contained another important formality beyond the notice requirement. To remain valid for longer than 28 years, a copyright had to be registered and renewed in the US Copyright Office. Fast-forward to 1960, when the copyright in *Lunch atop a Skyscraper* could have been renewed for a term lasting until 2027. And indeed, a diligent researcher will find that the *Herald Tribune* renewed the copyright in the October 2, 1932, issue of its newspaper on page 365 of the 1960 renewal records.[14]

Whether this 1960 filing by the newspaper renewed the copyright in *Lunch atop a Skyscraper* (as opposed to merely renewing the copyright in the newspaper) is one of the nastier and more obscure questions of copyright law. As noted earlier, courts found that a newspaper could preserve a copyright in a photo by providing a general notice at the front of the paper, but significant doubts exist as to whether a newspaper's renewal certificate similarly preserves the photo's copyright beyond the expiration date of 28 years set by the 1909 Act.

A whimsical recent case, however, sheds much light on just what the *New York Herald Tribune* renewed in 1960. Lovers of CBS's number-one-rated television smash, *The Big Bang Theory*, will recognize the lyrics and music to a song that has the power to magically calm the famously difficult Dr. Sheldon Cooper:

Soft Kitty
Warm Kitty
Little Ball of Fur
Happy Kitty

Sleepy Kitty

Purr, Purr, Purr

The lyrics were initially included in a collection of musical compositions entitled *Songs for Nursery School*, published with proper notice in 1937 by Willis Music Group, whose copyrights are now owned by Warner Chappell Music. The copyright in the *collection* of songs was renewed in 1965, but no individual certificate was filed for the lyrics to "Soft Kitty."

Sound familiar?

The daughters of the lyricist, Edith Newlin, brought suit in 2015, claiming CBS owed them royalties.[15] CBS replied that the Willis Music Group's renewal certificate did not operate to renew the song's copyright in favor of the daughters. The renewal preserved only Willis's copyright in the collection as a whole, essentially protecting the company only from someone ripping off all or most of its compilation. Willis was not a party to the suit against CBS because it did not own the copyright in the individual songs in its collection, like "Soft Kitty." Willis never obtained the rights in the song from Newlin, just a nonexclusive license to reprint it.

The court found that Newlin's daughters had an impossible case to make. Under the 1909 Act, the renewal by Willis Music of the songbook copyright would protect an individual song *only if* the song had been sold to Willis Music. So, if Newlin had transferred the song to Willis, it would still be under copyright. But this was not the case, and, in any event, a transfer wouldn't help the daughters since a prior sale by their mom would mean they did not inherit the song.

The daughters responded that their mother had not assigned rights to Willis. Their mother, and later her estate, had always owned the song. In that case, replied the court, the mother or daughters could have and should have renewed the copyright in the song at the proper time. Without a renewal in their name, the song fell into the public domain 28 years after publication. "Soft Kitty" is a harsh mistress for authors and artists claiming that a renewal filed by the copyright owner in a collective work, like a periodical, newspaper, or a book of songs, somehow benefits the contributor rather than the renewer.

The "Soft Kitty" decision makes sense, especially in the photographic context. Photographers were at the mercy of newspapers and periodicals, which refused to preserve the artists' rights by placing the necessary notice on each published photo. So, allowing a magazine or newspaper's general copyright notice to preserve the rights of photographers from extinction was very fair and equitable. However, neither law nor practice impeded photographers from renewing their copyrights. Having benefited from the notice fiction that preserved their works from falling into the public domain upon publication, photographers (or other artistic contributors) bore the responsibility for filing their own renewals 28 years later, just like all other copyright owners.

Returning to *Lunch atop a Skyscraper*, my search of Copyright Office records reveals no renewal certificates filed by Charles Ebbets in the relevant years of 1960 or 1961. We can assume that Ebbets, like most other photographers of his era, decided that 28 years of protection was enough and chose not to file. In fact, only 227 renewal certificates were filed for "photographs and artwork" in 1960[16] and only 193 in 1961.[17]

The foregoing might give the impression that the photograph is clearly in the public domain, and it probably is, but we first must consider the status of two other parties: the *New York Herald Tribune* and whoever commissioned the photographs for the Rockefeller Center.

First, the newspaper could have received an assignment from either Ebbets or his employer (assuming it was a work-for-hire). If so, according to the "Soft Kitty" case, the paper's renewal of its copyright in the October 2, 1932, Sunday edition, would have renewed its copyright in the photo. No assignment from Ebbets to the *Herald Tribune* was ever filed in the Copyright Office,[18] but an assignment need not be filed to be valid between the parties. So, who knows whether an assignment was made? Personally, I doubt it.

Moreover, even if the newspaper received an assignment, the *Herald Tribune* wound down its affairs and disappeared in 1966. Richard Kluger details the paper's 1958 acquisition by John Hay Whitney (a former US ambassador to the UK) and Whitney Communications Corporation, which was then succeeded by Whitcom Investments, Inc.[19] A 1991 story in the *New York Times* states that the *Times* and the *Washington Post* acquired Whitcom's stake in another paper, the *International Herald Tribune*, and perhaps that deal included an assignment of old *New York Herald Tribune* copyrights.[20] If so, no record of any assignment can be found in the Copyright Office.[21] The University of Texas owns the physical newspaper archives of the *New York Herald Tribune*,[22] but that does not mean it took assignments of the copyrights. In other words, if Ebbets sold the copyright in the photo to the newspaper (which seems unlikely), there is no easy way to follow the chain of title.

Finally, the original party that commissioned the work (probably the Rockefeller Center) could have claimed to be the original owner. If the Rockefeller Center were the original owner under the "instance and expense" test discussed earlier, it never filed a renewal during the relevant period for any photographs. Of course, if the Rockefeller Center were the original owner, it might have transferred the copyright to some unknown third party that filed a renewal certificate. Unfortunately, you need to know the title of a work or its owner to search the Copyright Office records. The photo was published without a title, and we have no way to trace the name of a hypothetical transferee of the Rockefeller Center.

We can see how the US copyright system is destined to create orphans like *Lunch atop a Skyscraper.*

Given the likelihood that the work is in the public domain, why don't people just use the photo of *Lunch atop a Skyscraper* and humbly offer to pay a reasonable fee to anyone who shows up with a valid renewal certificate? Wouldn't the collection of a licensing fee satisfy the hypothetical owner? Unfortunately, the Copyright Act provides for special, extra-compensatory damages for copyright owners who register and renew their copyrights. An infringer could be ordered to pay between $500 to $30,000 in statutory damages, even if the copyright owner has not lost any profits. US law (unlike Canadian and UK law) provides no safe harbor for those who have done an exhaustive search and cannot determine who, if anyone, owns a copyright.

Do you feel lucky, punk?

I would like to think that a sensible judge would not hammer a user who has exhausted all means of finding the owner. In fact, I'm betting on it, given that I've included the photo in this book without paying anyone.

Unfortunately, the story of *Lunch atop a Skyscraper* is repeated over and over as users search in vain for owners of copyrights in photographs. Consider the statistics on copyright renewal in the category of "artwork and photographs" (table 1.1).[23]

TABLE 1.1. Number of Photographical Renewals.

YEAR	NUMBER OF WORKS RENEWED
1968	382
1969	285
1970	251
1971	379
1972	390
1973	658
	2,345

Source: US Copyright Office.

I chose records from 1968 to 1972 because those were the years when photographs from 1940 to 1945 should have been renewed. We can safely assume that millions of photographs were taken during the turbulent years encompassing World War II. And yet, copyrights in only 2,345 pieces of "Artwork and Photography" were renewed by their owners (and many of these renewals were of artwork other than photographs).

Of course, this doesn't mean that all but 2,345 works from this period fell into the public domain. Copyrights in photos taken by employees of magazines and newspapers were preserved when the magazines and newspapers properly renewed their copyrights in the collective works (and filed in the Copyright Office under "periodicals" and not "photographs"). Other copyrights formally assigned from independent photographers to periodicals or newspapers were also renewed when the certificate for the collective work was filed.

In other words, we can be pretty sure that millions of photographs from 1940 to 1945 fell into the public domain and only thousands of copyrights were preserved. But how can we tell the difference between protected and unprotected works?

We can't.

First of all, the renewal records of photographs from that era are filed under the names of the copyright owners (who might not be the photographers). Since photographers were seldom credited by periodicals at that time, the odds of learning the name of the photographer to begin tracking title are close to zero.

Why not just carry the photograph you want to use directly to the Copyright Office and ask whether its copyright was ever registered or renewed? That's the approach I take when I need a replacement part for a repair project. I bring the part to a hardware store, hand it to a clerk, and say, "give me one of these."

The Copyright Office doesn't work like that. It does not have a file cabinet full of photographs for you to look through and compare. Without the name of the copyright owner or title of the work, the Copyright Office cannot help you.

The renewal records give the names of renewing owners and also provide some titles of the renewed works, but that doesn't help searchers much. For example, on page 135 of the renewal records for 1968 (covering works from 1940), you will learn that Georg B. Luks renewed his copyright in a photograph of "a guitar." If you bring a 1940 photo of a guitar to the Copyright Office, can the records tell you whether your photo is Luks's? Absolutely not.

To its credit, the Copyright Office is trying to help. It supports "orphan works" legislation that would permit the legal use of a work when a reasonable search has failed to identify the copyright owner.[24] Such legislation would free up millions of photographs and would require users to pay a reasonable royalty in cases where the copyright owner comes out of the woodwork. Proposals for such sensible legislation have languished in a dysfunctional Congress for almost a decade.

Interestingly, the UK has created a consumer-friendly website that provides potential licensees with tips on searching for orphan works and with advice on when they have done enough to proceed with legally using the work of an unfindable owner.[25]

Secret Property Rights

We should contemplate the possibility that the US system as just described is unconstitutional. Imagine a woman fishing, ready to cast her line into a lake. A game warden approaches and signals that she stop.

"Be careful," the government official explains, "some of the fish in the lake belong to the public and are fair game to catch and eat. Others are privately owned, and if you eat them, you will be fined between $500 and $30,000."

"Okay," she replies, "that's fine. I'll just release the privately owned fish back into the water and only eat the public domain fish." She pauses for a moment. "How do I tell which fish are privately owned and which fish are fair game?"

"You can't," replies Warden Kafka with a menacing laugh. "Congress declares some of these fish to be private property, but the government will not tell you which fish they are!"

Although one cannot find Supreme Court cases precisely on point—mostly because governmental registration schemes are usually logical, efficient, and effective—it's plausible that enforcing unknowable secret property rights threatens a core due process right guaranteed by the Constitution. In a very real sense, the public domain is our property, owned by the people of the US. The inability of the Copyright Office to tell us what we can use deprives us of our property without due process of law. The federal government maintains easily searchable registries of who owns patents (https://www.uspto.gov/patents-application-process/search-patents), aircraft (https://registry.faa.gov/aircraftinquiry/), and liens on railroad rolling stock (https://prod.stb.gov/proceedings-actions/recordations-main/). It can solve the notice problem if it has the political will.

CHAPTER TWO

BLURRED LINES AND BUMMED MUSICIANS

(more herein on difficult-to-discern rights)

In 2013, Robin Thicke and Pharrell Williams wrote, produced, and performed "a smug turd of a pop song" that, in the words of the *Village Voice*, "has ruined the music industry."[1] The song was "Blurred Lines," and it came with a video featuring Thicke and Williams cavorting with suggestively clad dancers who were meant to illustrate the song's tag line, "You're a good girl; I know you want it."[2] The song spent 17 weeks at the top of the Billboard charts, and by April 2020, the video had been viewed more than 656 million times on YouTube.

The song is not infamous because of its insensitive treatment of women (well, that's some of it—the *Village Voice* described the song as "kinda rapey"). The threat to the music industry comes not from offensive lyrics but because Thicke and Williams were successfully sued by the estate of Marvin Gaye for infringing his song "Got to Give It Up."[3]

Take a moment and listen to both songs, preferably by using iTunes, Spotify, or Pandora to avoid watching the insipid and sleazy "Blurred Lines" video posted on YouTube.

You will hear a similarity of "vibe" between the two songs. After all, Thicke and Williams stated in their depositions that they were inspired by Marvin Gaye and wanted to create a song that captured the musical atmospherics of his genre and era. The lyrics are different and so are the very basic melodies, although melody is secondary to both works. Both songs are primarily about rhythm and instrumentation, with both relying heavily on clanging cowbells, a relentless beat, and a good bit of mumbled voicing in the background. Gaye's falsetto is quite distinctive and sets his song apart, but if you focus on the cowbells and the beat, you may be tempted to say the songs sound alike.

The jury was more than tempted by what they heard—they awarded Marvin Gaye's heirs $7 million, the largest music infringement award to date.[4] Exploring how this judgment has the potential to "ruin the music industry" leads to the conclusion that major reform of music copyright law may be necessary.

To see the need for reform, we need to make a brief foray into the law of music copyright infringement. What law is a jury supposed to apply when determining whether one song infringes another? The key instruction comes from a 1946 case involving a bizarre lawsuit against American composer and popular music superstar Cole Porter ("Night and Day," "Begin the Beguine," "I've Got You Under My Skin," "My Heart Belongs to Daddy," etc.). Porter was sued by Ira Arnstein, a paranoid rival who claimed that Porter's "stooges" had stolen his tunes. Arnstein brought many music infringement lawsuits and inevitably lost, but in *Arnstein v. Porter* he set a precedent on appeal that has haunted composers ever since.

In evaluating his claim, the Second Circuit Court of Appeals described the legal standard for music copyright infringement as follows:

> Whether defendant took from plaintiff's works so much of what is pleasing to the ears of lay listeners, who comprise the audience of whom such popular music is composed, that the defendant appropriated something which belongs to the plaintiff.[5]

Imagine being a juror hearing this instruction. First, you are supposed to listen not through your own ears but through the ears of "lay listeners" of "popular music." Then, you must identify how much was taken by the defendant, but that question is not simple. You must focus on what is "pleasing" to a lay listener. Was too much of *that* stuff taken? You will also be told that you should ignore any similarities in the songs that spring from the same public domain source. For example, if both the defendant and the plaintiff took 10 measures from a public domain French folk song and that is the reason the songs sound similar to each other, then you should find the defendant not liable.

Of course, expert witnesses will "help" you make your decision. The first part of their testimony will focus on whether the defendant actually took anything at all because independent creation is a complete defense to infringement. A lot of songs, especially pop songs, sound alike simply because they are in the same genre and use the same chord progression. Rock songs, for example, usually proceed with a harmonic pattern of I, IV, V, I. (Check out Axis of Awesome's "Four Chord Song," a mash-up of popular songs that all have the same familiar-sounding structure.)[6] The first wave of testimony will consider whether the two songs sound the same for reasons other than copying.

If copying is shown, then experts will testify whether what was copied from the plaintiff's song was protectable. The copied bit might be trite and unoriginal, or perhaps the plaintiff borrowed it from some other source. Is the borrowed bit pleasing to the ears of lay listeners? How much was borrowed? Copyright law has a doctrine of *de minimis* borrowing, which allows musicians to take a little bit from a copyrighted work without permission.

Unfortunately, the defendant's and plaintiff's experts are likely to disagree on all of these issues.

If possible, the "Blurred Lines" decision made matters even worse. Composers were fairly certain before the litigation that just borrowing the "vibe" of a song, without copying its lyrics or melody, was permissible. That's why Thicke and Williams were so willing to admit their motivations and fight to the bitter end. Their lawyers probably told them, with good reason, that they were sure to succeed.

Now, imagine a lawyer advising a concerned composer who does not want to violate anyone's copyright. If the client-musician is sued and the case goes to trial, can anyone predict what the jury will do? How can a lawyer confidently advise a client?

Attorneys could just advise composers not to copy at all, but you might as well tell them not to compose.[7] If the client is Bruce Springsteen, he has to use the I, IV, V, I chord structure he heard growing up. If the client is a country music star, she has to sing about trucks, drinking, cheating, and dusty dirt roads. And rap performers? They have an especially limited set of rhythms from which to borrow.

Composers have always looked to their peers for inspiration. Igor Stravinsky once said, "Good composers borrow; great composers steal,"[8] and he wasn't just talking about his contemporaries. From medieval monks to renaissance composers to Bach to Handel to Mozart and onward, the frequency of musical borrowing has been documented exhaustively by musicologists of all genres.[9] Consider this quote from Elvis Costello:

> I went to Rock On, the secondhand record shop in Camden Town and bought every old Stax 45 that they had on their shelf and carried them home to plunder. . . . Almost everything we needed to arrange the new songs was pilfered from that pile of old records. A lot of pop music has come out of people failing to copy their model and accidentally creating something new. . . . Our cack-handed, wired-up attempts to play like bands we'd heard on Motown and Atlantic compilations were just enough to get us away from our clichés.[10]

So, a lawyer cannot realistically advise a composer to never borrow from another musician. This is what makes the current situation so frustrating: how much is okay to borrow?

Consider another recent lawsuit. Led Zeppelin toured in the late sixties with Spirit, a successful Los Angeles rock band fronted by Randy Wolfe, a.k.a. Randy California. Over the years, some listeners have heard similarities between California's guitar work on an instrumental piece called "Taurus" and the famous acoustic intro played by Jimmy Page on Zeppelin's later epic "Stairway to Heaven." Long after California died while saving his son from drowning off the coast of Hawaii, his estate brought suit against Led Zeppelin for allegedly ripping off "Taurus."

Anyone taking a moment to listen to the two songs will find the claim of close similarity a bit of a head-scratcher,[11] as did the jury, who found in favor of Led Zeppelin. Despite the pro-defendant verdict, the case does not make client counseling much easier. Led Zeppelin spent more than $800,000 defending the lawsuit. Sure, a jury agreed that Jimmy Page did not take too much of "what is pleasing to the ears of lay listeners," but few composers or performers can afford this sort of cost to fight off the baseless claims that the *Arnstein* test invites.[12]

Unfortunately, the joy of Led Zeppelin fans was short lived. The Ninth Circuit found an unrelated problem with the jury instructions and remanded to the district court for a new trial, although the Ninth Circuit recently reinstated the initial verdict.[13]

One further important aspect of the case: Randy California never sued Led Zeppelin or asked for compensation or a writing credit. As a musician steeped in jazz, blues, and rock traditions, he undoubtedly borrowed as well. Listen to Spirit's biggest hit, *I Got a Line on You*, which has a heavy Cream/Jimi Hendrix vibe (California hung out with Hendrix as a teenager). We can surmise that California understood the interchange of musical ideas and was probably comfortable with Page's work on "Stairway to Heaven," which he had heard many times. The fact that California didn't object suggests that musicians are communal people, with a general understanding of how much borrowing is acceptable and how much is too much.

What if that understanding were the basis of law? What if the law of music infringement were not some whacky test focusing on lay listeners but rather incorporated the actual borrowing norms of communities of musicians?

The Case for Reform

What follows is an extended argument for why the lay-listener test should be junked and replaced with a rule that focuses on what musicians think is acceptable borrowing. Such a change would benefit composers and promote the production of music, which is what music copyright law should be about.

Note first that the US may already be required to defer to borrowing norms of musicians. In 1994, the US joined the Berne Convention for the Protection of Literary and Artistic Works. Congress takes adherence to the Berne treaty seriously and amended US copyright law in several ways to conform to its mandates. By joining the convention, the US promised to abide by article 10(1), which reads:

> It shall be permissible to make quotations from a work which has already been lawfully made available to the public, provided that their making is compatible with fair practice.

This language "compatible with fair practice" can plausibly be read to mandate deference to established borrowing norms.

The borrowing of notes by one musician from another is commonly called "quoting,"[14] and the drafting history article 10(1) makes it clear that "quotations" are not limited to verbal quotes of prose literature.[15] Second, each member state is required to ("shall") permit quoting. Third, and most important, the test for when quoting is permissible focuses directly on "fair practice." In other words, if pop performers and composers generally think that Robin Thicke and Pharrell Williams's attempt to capture the "vibe" of "Got to Give It Up" was consistent with fair practice in the pop/soul genre, then they should have had a valid defense to the charge of infringement by the Marvin Gaye estate.

The notion of deferring to professional or community norms may sound familiar because it's the core US negligence law. Consider medical malpractice. Your doctor is not automatically liable if something goes wrong during surgery. If the doctor followed the proper procedures and operated in accordance with accepted medical practice, the doctor has a defense, no matter how badly things turned out. The patient has the burden of proving that the doctor was negligent: that her behavior would be considered unreasonable by other doctors in her specialty.

The same goes for architects. If an apartment collapses during a minor earthquake, the building's designer is not automatically held liable. Maybe the contractor built it with poor materials. An architect is liable only when a building design fails to meet accepted architectural standards. If the building is designed in accordance with those norms, then the architect has a complete defense to a claim of negligent design, even if dozens of people were harmed by the building's collapse.

If we stick with architects for just a moment, we can see another example of the weirdness of copyright infringement law. Imagine an architect is sued for copyright infringement for borrowing part of another architect's design. How do we tell whether the architect has borrowed too much? Not surprisingly, architects borrow from each other all the time—just sit down with any house plans magazine from the supermarket and start counting the common features in the dwellings. If you spend enough time with the magazines, you can begin to guess architectural norms. Slavishly copying a competitor's striking new office building is not permissible; borrowing the placement of a kitchen island in a residence is apparently fine.

Unfortunately for architects (but consistent with the approach taken in music cases), courts do not defer to professional borrowing norms in design

infringement cases. Instead of focusing on whether an accused architect is borrowing in the same way that architects usually borrow, the court may ask the
jury whether the defendant took the "look and feel" of the plaintiff's design.[16]

Good luck predicting how a case will come out under the "look and feel"
standard.

Architects and composers deserve to have more predictability in their creative lives. In fact, fear of liability could deter creation, defeating the main justification for copyright in the first place!

Most architects and composers undergo some sort of training in their profession. Architects usually have formal academic training in addition to meeting state-imposed professional qualifications, while musicians are socialized
formally and informally, with or without university degrees. Musicians learn
by observing and listening, by studying intently what has come before and by
closely attending to their teachers and role models. Neither profession develops
its creative intuition in a vacuum. Learning is communal, and borrowing from
others is not only inevitable but necessary socialization.

An architect designing a new building or a composer writing a new song
will strive to be innovative, but carving out a bit of original space is a daunting
task. So much has come before! So many houses and office blocks, so many pop
songs and country ballads. Crafting even a nugget of creativity is praiseworthy,
and, not surprisingly, it is those nuggets that architects and musicians believe
should be most protected. The rest of the materials needed to design a house
or sing the blues are freely passed along from one artist to the next, from one
generation to another.

Why shouldn't the law defer to shared understandings (where they exist) of
the appropriate level of borrowing?

Interestingly, copyright law more or less already defers to the borrowing
norms of computer programmers. People who write software are constantly
borrowing from each other. In fact, some of the most valuable software invites
copying. Do you use a Linux operating system? Does your place of employment
use Apache software on its server? Have you ever browsed with Mozilla, or do
you use Open Office instead of Microsoft Word? Programmers are constantly
making enormous amounts of code available for others to copy outright, imitate,
or improve on (often with some restrictions; e.g., if you improve the Linux kernel,

you are contractually restricted from charging people for your improvements). One likely reason the software industry exploded so quickly was the ethic of sharing among programmers.

When it came time for Congress to evaluate whether computer software should be protected the same way as literary works, programmers expressed deep concerns about expanding copyright law to cover their profession. The people whom copyright law would protect opined that it might stifle the very creative activity that it was supposed to nurture.[17]

Although Congress decided to define "literary works" to include software, the judiciary quickly intervened and radically narrowed the scope of protection to a level that satisfied most in the programming community. In *Computer Associates v. Altai*, the Second Circuit did not apply a "lay observer" test to a line of code, adopting instead an innovative abstraction-filtration-comparison test to maintain programmers' ability to copy without worrying too hard about liability. Under *Altai*, a court will identify any ideas present in the plaintiff's program and leave them unprotected. Then, it will filter out aspects of the plaintiff's program that are driven by efficiency (a prime programming concern) or external factors like compatibility requirements. The court will also filter out routine programming motifs and anything borrowed from the public domain.

After all this filtering, the plaintiff's "golden nugget" (the *Altai* court's term, not mine) is then compared to the defendant's program. If the golden nugget is big enough and the defendant took too much of it, then the defendant will be found liable.[18] *Altai* protects most programmers from liability unless they commit outright piracy, counterfeiting whole programs or large chunks of programs. Today, the best way to describe computer copyright law is to say that it protects programmers from pirates but gives them very little protection from their competitors. This is pretty much the way programmers like it.

Why not give musicians the level of protection *they* would like to have? Why shouldn't musical experts, steeped in the historical borrowing norms of each musical genre, determine when a composer or performer has crossed a line?

Some details would need to be ironed out. Not all genres are equally tolerant of borrowing—jazz artists, for example, are particularly bold borrowers. And what should be done about inter-genre borrowing, like a hip-hop artist who loops two measures from a copyrighted symphony? Despite difficulties in application, my guess is that musicians would rather be judged by a panel of peers referring to historical borrowing practices than by a jury applying the infamous lay-listener test.

However, neither Congress nor the courts can adopt this proposal because the Constitution requires a jury trial in litigation. Perhaps courts should keep juries but dump the lay-listener test and adopt a defense based on the language of article 10(1) of Berne. Judges could tell juries that "[i]t shall be permissible to make quotations from a work which has already been lawfully made available to the public, provided that their making is compatible with fair practice." Courts, however, are not major engines of innovation in this field, and perhaps they shouldn't be.

The best and most effective protection for musicians and composers could come via contract law. Viral contract law! Major musical outlets (YouTube, Spotify, Pandora, Amazon Music, iTunes, etc.) and collecting societies (ASCAP, SESAC, BMI, SoundExchange, etc.) could easily include in their form contracts with composers and performers the following clause: "All claims of copyright infringement made by signatories to this agreement shall be settled through binding arbitration before a panel of _____ (musicians?) chosen by _____ (the parties?). Borrowing compatible with fair musical practice shall be a defense to a claim of infringement."

The most natural proponent for such reform would be ASCAP, the American Society of Composers and Publishers, which could fill in the blanks above by establishing a trusted roster of musicians, musicologists, and music historians who could serve as neutral arbitrators. ASCAP could also determine the method whereby a panel would be chosen. A major player like ASCAP could standardize procedures and kick-start a system that would take juries out of the equation and put the fate of musicians in the hands of musicians.

Nonetheless, policymakers should consider whether self-regulation might have a dark side. For good reasons, the law does not inevitably defer to community norms. A brief consideration of the circumstances where deference is dangerous confirms that allowing "borrowing compatible with fair practice" should be a legitimate defense in music cases.

Situations When Deferring to Local Norms Can
Be Contrary to the Public Interest

1. Consider the pharmacists in your hometown. Imagine that their consistent professional practice is to talk on the phone every morning and agree to fix high prices for drugs. This behavior is anticompetitive and against the public interest. It is also per se illegal under US antitrust law. Should these sleazebags have a defense based on their historically consistent professional practice? Of course not. They should go to jail.

2. Consider also activities so naturally dangerous that we want only a limited number of people to engage in them. In several older cases involving the storage of dynamite or nitroglycerine, courts decided to apply a rule of strict liability. If someone blows up the neighborhood, then that person is always liable for the damage. Period. The courts generally refused to recognize a (posthumous?) defense of "I handled the nitroglycerine in a manner consistent with professional nitro-handling norms." We want people to think twice or more about storing hazardous materials. By making people strictly liable and denying a reasonable practice defense, the law seeks to limit dangerous behavior.

3. Finally, courts will not defer to professional norms when outsiders have better information about the consequences of the behavior in question. Consider an automobile company debating whether to install air bags as a safety mechanism in the days before they were required. The company has some data from a limited number of crash tests, but the tests are expensive to perform and cannot comprehensively measure all risks. The limited data available to the firm suggest that air bags might not be a cost-effective protection measure. If other car manufacturers come to the same conclusion, then a consistent practice of "no air bags" might become the norm. At the same time, the US government has gathered decades' worth of statistics and analyses of hundreds of accidents around the country that prove that air bags are a cost-effective—indeed vital—safety measure.

In such a case, do we want a court to defer to private norms when a public agency has a superior ability to conduct risk analysis? In several areas of law, courts have been unwilling to defer to professional norms when the profession should incorporate valuable new information in its decision making.

At this point, we should ask whether any of these three cautionary tales suggests that deferring to the historical borrowing practices of performers and composers would pose similar threats to public welfare. It's hard to imagine potential problems, especially since even the most sophisticated experts cannot tell us what the optimal level of borrowing is.

If musicians adopt a norm that discourages borrowing and encourages more licensing activity, then they are the ones who bear the additional transaction costs. If musicians adopt a norm that encourages borrowing, then they are willingly sharing and bearing the costs of that activity. The public welfare could certainly be affected by these normative shifts, but with no outsider better positioned to evaluate the utility of the norm, why not let musicians themselves decide?

Coda: Data on Musical Borrowing

This book strives to be data-driven, so it would be remiss to ignore the only empirical study that examines the pitfalls of the *Arnstein* lay-listener approach.

In 2012, Jamie Lund assembled a series of mock juries, played them music, and gave them the jury instruction asking them to compare two musical works. Her experiment was prompted by the disturbing (and common) practice of judges in music infringement cases playing sound recordings to juries.

What's odd about playing a recording of the plaintiff's music to the jury and then playing the defendant's music?

The infringement scenarios that we have discussed so far do not involve the copying of a sound recording. Those cases are usually straightforward and thus seldom get reported in the case law. Anyone who pirates a CD or a vinyl disk or an mp3 file is an infringer. Boring. If, on the other hand, someone makes a sound-alike recording (imagine me doing an amazingly exact imitation of Bruno Mars singing "Grenade"), then he is immune from liability. The copyright act specifically states that a sound recording copyright cannot be violated by mere imitation.

Now that's more interesting! This means that music copyright infringement cases are almost always about whether the defendant infringed the underlying musical composition, that is, the sheet music, *not* the recording of the song. Consider the Beatles classic "Yesterday." By 2014, it had been legally recorded more than 4,000 times by almost as many artists. If someone writes or plays a song suspiciously similar to "Yesterday" without a license and is sued by Sir Paul McCartney, the sole issue will be whether the defendant's song infringes

McCartney's sheet music, the written-down version of the song. The thousands of recordings of the song are irrelevant.

So, in a music copyright infringement case, a jury must compare what the defendant has done with what the plaintiff wrote down. Unfortunately, most jurors don't read music very well, so handing them a visual copy of the plaintiff's composition may elicit only confused looks. For this reason, courts allow recordings of the plaintiff's song to be played along with the defendant's work. In the "Blurred Lines" case, for example, the jury was allowed to hear Marvin Gaye's recording of "Got to Give It Up."

Lund's experiments demonstrated the problem of playing music for juries: they have a hard time determining whether two songs sound alike because of the way they are performed or whether they sound alike because the defendant copied too much of the plaintiff's sheet music. To repeat, it's perfectly legal for two recordings to sound alike. Under the Copyright Act, the issue is whether the defendant borrowed too much of the plaintiff's composition.

Lund demonstrated how easily juries can be manipulated into finding that two songs are similar (or dissimilar) merely by changing how they are played. One experiment was based on music from a real case, in which Mariah Carey was sued by Seth Swirskey, who claimed Carey's hit "Thank God I Found You" improperly borrowed from his composition "One of Those Love Songs."[19] One set of subjects heard both compositions played in a similar fashion, sharing similar tempo, orchestration, key, and style. These subjects overwhelmingly (87 percent) found the Swirskey and Carey songs to be similar.

A different group of subjects heard the Swirskey and Carey compositions played in different tempos, orchestration, key, and style. The notes played were exactly the same as those played to the first group of listeners, but this time only 28 percent of the subjects found the songs to be similar, *even though the notes of both songs played to the audience were identical.*

As explained above, the only music at issue is the notes as the plaintiff wrote them on the page. How an artist chosen by the plaintiff (in the real case, the all-female R&B group Xscape) actually recorded those notes is supposed to be completely irrelevant under the law. Lund's experiment shows why. Jurors will be unduly influenced by factors like similarity in musical style, which is unprotected by copyright law.

One has some sympathy for courts because they cannot realistically throw sheet music at jurors and ask them to compare written compositions. Playing the plaintiff's song seems to be inevitable, which provides another reason to endorse a system in which people who can read music are asked to objectively evaluate the amount of permissibility borrowing in light of historical practice.

CHAPTER THREE

KURT VONNEGUT, *THE LION KING*, AND HOW AUTHORS GET THEIR GROOVE BACK

TIME FOR A POSITIVE STORY ABOUT COPYRIGHT! Copyright may last too long, and owners of old photos may be ridiculously (and maybe even unconstitutionally) difficult to find, but authors' rights legislation is a step in the right direction. Legislatures have occasionally shown concern for authors who make bad deals and risk poverty while their publishers get rich. In England, at the turn of the last century, Parliament was so embarrassed by the specter of Charles Dickens's grandchildren going hungry that it provided for all authors' copyrights to revert from publishers to their heirs 25 years after their deaths. As we will see, this rights reversion provision in the 1911 Imperial Copyright Act applied to all UK and Commonwealth authors, not just Dickens.

The US also has a scheme (actually three) that enables authors to get their copyrights back, even if they initially signed them away in blood in front of 20 genuflecting bishops.

Authors of post-1978 US works can terminate any transfer of copyright 35 years after the transfer. Remember the Village People's campy hit "Y.M.C.A."? Its author, Victor Willis (who was the policeman in the group), got back his copyright in the song in 2013, which allowed him to renegotiate his music publishing deal, to collect royalties from its adaptation in other media, and to use it as the basis of new derivative works.[1]

As of 2020, the copyrights to thousands of valuable compositions and books from 1978 to 1985 have been subject to the author's termination right, with countless more copyrights reverting to authors every year.

For works published before 1978, the reversion scheme is quite a bit more complicated. For these works, an author who transferred a copyright and then lived more than 28 years after the publication of the work is stuck with the contract for an *additional* 28 years (and so are the heirs), for total of 56 years. At year 56, however, the survivors can obtain the copyright, and those failing to exercise that right get another opportunity in year 75. For example, the copyright of James Michener's (1907–97) novel *Hawaii* (1957) was eligible for recapture by his heirs in 2013.

If the author of a pre-1978 work died *before* year 28, then the heirs automatically got the copyright back in year 28. For example, Margaret Mitchell published *Gone with the Wind* in 1936, but she was killed by a drunk driver in Atlanta in 1949. Therefore, her heirs had the right to regain the copyright 28 years after publication, in 1964. The copyrights to bestsellers like *Lolita* (1958), *Atlas Shrugged* (1957), and *Dr. Zhivago* (1958) were all similarly eligible for reversion to the heirs of Vladimir Nabokov (1899–1977), Ayn Rand (1905–82), and Boris Pasternak (1890–1960), respectively, in the 28th year after publication.

In the Jungle, the Mighty Jungle, the Lion Sleeps Tonight

The most striking story of rights reversion is the "infa-Mouse" case brought by the heirs of South African singer and composer Solomon Linda (1909–62) against the Walt Disney Corporation.

Linda sang soprano with the Evening Birds, a successful group who performed mostly in Johannesburg beer halls starting in the 1920s. In 1939, they were "discovered" and recorded several songs, including "Mbube," a tune written by Linda that forms the backbone of the song we know now as "The Lion Sleeps Tonight (Wimoweh)." According to the *New York Times*, Linda received less than one dollar for the copyright to the song, which soon became the first South African recording to sell 100,000 copies.[2]

In 1949, folksinger Pete Seger heard the Evening Birds' recording of "Mbube." He loved the song and performed it frequently with his group, the Weavers, who also recorded it. For an unknown reason, he converted the words "Mbube" (Zulu for "lion") into "Wimoweh" (English for "Oops, I didn't know I was ripping off a poor African dude"), and the lyric change stuck.

Although the Kingston Trio had a minor hit with the song, the recording made by the Tokens in 1961 became a number-one hit and spawned hundreds of cover versions across the globe, drilling the doo wop rhythm and high soprano overlay into the consciousness of generations of listeners.

No wonder Disney wanted the tune in its 1994 movie *The Lion King*! Is there a more famous song about lions? Keep in mind that Mumford & Sons' "Little Lion Man" had not yet been recorded, and the *Wizard of Oz* soundtrack gives equal time to "tigers and bears, oh my!"

Disney, of course, was very aware of copyright law and got permission to use the song from Abilene Music, which appeared to own the legal rights through a series of assignments. All was well from Disney's perspective until an article in *Rolling Stone* revealed the embarrassingly small compensation that Linda and his heirs had received from the song's exploitation.[3] The family had always been very poor, and one of Linda's daughters had died of malnutrition as a child. Owen Dean, formerly the Mostert Chair in Intellectual Property Law at Stellenbosch University (where I'm currently writing this chapter), decided to press the case of Linda's heirs against Disney for greater compensation.

Luckily for Linda's heirs, Dean remembered the 1911 UK Imperial Copyright Act and its provision for reverting copyrights to an author's heirs 25 years after the death of the author.

Although South Africa ceased being an English colony in 1910, UK copyright law remained in force until South Africa drafted its own statute in 1965. That new statute abolished the Dickens-inspired reversion provision, but only for future works, retaining reversion of rights for works published before 1965. The Dickens provision survives similarly in other Commonwealth countries: for works published before 1987 in Singapore, before 1969 in Australia, and before 1965 in New Zealand.

The math is not hard to do. Solomon Linda's "Mbube" was published well before 1965, and he died in 1962. His heirs, then, became owners of his copyrights in 1987, seven years before the premier of *The Lion King*. Although earlier assignments made by Linda's daughters complicated the straightforwardness of the claims, Disney settled with the family for an undisclosed but presumably substantial sum. After all, with a lifetime gross box office of almost $430 million (making *The Lion King* the top-grossing G-rated movie of all time [since overtaken by *Toy Story 4*]),[4] Disney would have been foolish to let a jury determine the value added to the movie by Timon and Poomba's endearing duet of the song, especially given the impoverished state of Linda's family.

American Reversion, Vonnegut Style

The US statutes that allow authors to get back their copyrights are augmented by a federal court decision prompted by Kurt Vonnegut's desire to see novels like *Slaughterhouse 5*, *Cat's Cradle*, and the *Sirens of Titan* in e-book form. In the early days of digital publishing, years before the appearance of the Kindle, Nook, or iPad Reader, Vonnegut's publisher, Random House, was worried that e-books would be subjected to the same sort of massive piracy suffered by the music industry and was therefore slow to exploit the digital market. So, upstart Rosetta Books approached Vonnegut and William Styron (*Sophie's Choice*) and offered to publish e-books of their works. Vonnegut and Styron agreed, and Rosetta was sued for copyright infringement by Random House.

Random House looked to have an open and shut case. After all, it had contracts signed by both authors transferring all rights to their stories "in book form" to the publisher. The contracts, however, were signed at a time when digital publishing was the stuff of science fiction. The contracts did not say anything specific about e-book rights. Random House argued that the reason for the broad assignment of "all rights in book form" was to cover all future means of publication, especially those not specifically anticipated by the parties. Its argument was simple: a story in digital format is "in book form."[5]

In a landmark decision, the court held otherwise, finding, perhaps counterintuitively, that an e-book is not "in book form."[6] After the case, many authors around America (at least those with Random House–like language in their publishing contracts) were surprised to learn that they retained the digital rights to their stories.

The decision in *Random House v. Rosetta Books* is functionally a rights-reversion story. Many authors who assumed that they had signed away their rights to the e-book market suddenly got those rights back. So, in the US, we have three major routes by which authors can wrest their copyrights back from publishers: (1) for pre-1978 works, authors or their heirs can get a copyright back in year 56 or 75 after publication; (2) for post-1978 works, authors or heirs can get a copyright back in year 35 after a transfer; and (3) for many older works covered by a vaguely worded contract, authors can immediately assert their digital rights. This third option, however, is likely to apply only to pre-2002 works because after *Rosetta* was decided publishers wrote contracts clearly claiming digital rights.

What Happens When Authors Get Their Groove Back

Although the original rationale for giving authors a second bite at the apple was highly paternalistic (to protect them from making bad contractual decisions), some commentators have suggested alternative justifications for reversion rights. Economists, in particular, seek a more compelling justification for denying publishers of post-1978 works the ability to purchase rights that last longer than 35 years: what if reversionary rights were good for the public, in addition to being good for authors and their families?

Some economists speculate that transferring rights from initial publishers back to authors might result in out-of-print books reappearing.[7] Maybe, under some circumstances, authors are better than publishers at making books available to the public. The "disappeared" books from the twentieth century described in the introduction might make a partial comeback if the copyrights in those books were restored to their authors.

Initially, this seems like an odd notion, given that publishers should have a profit motive to bring books back into print. Unfortunately, the book publishing industry has been creakingly inefficient for some time. A trio of Carnegie-Mellon researchers recently concluded that in the e-book market alone (currently about one-third of the book market), publishers are leaving approximately $780 million on the table by keeping titles out of print.[8]

Why? Part of the answer might be simple inertia—the reliance on business models developed in the predigital era were never updated. For example, some major publishers offer only books that are projected to sell 1,000 to 5,000 copies a year, even if they could make a profit on fewer sales. The most likely explanation for not exploiting marginally profitable titles involves reputation costs. Big publishers like Random House cultivate a reputation for publishing bestselling titles from well-known authors. Books that sell only a couple hundred copies a year? Well, those pickings are best left to small (sniff!) independent presses that are forced to work with lesser-known authors. A large publishing house may decide to leave some profit on the table for fear of compromising its reputation. For example, Burberry recently burned $37 million in merchandise rather than sell outside its business model to downscale retailers.[9]

In any event, the hypothesis that authors will do a better job of getting books back into print is testable because many US books are already eligible for reversion. For example, works from 1950 to 1961 became eligible for reversion between 2006 and 2018 under the 56-year rule. Works from 1978 to 1982 became eligible for reversion between 2013 and 2018 under the 35-year rule. Finally, after *Rosetta,* the digital rights in many books clearly vested in authors in 2002. The in-print status of reversion-eligible books can be compared to the status of books whose copyrights are still controlled by the original publisher.

In the US, a single author may have books governed by multiple reversion rules. Consider James Clavell (1921–94), whose wildly successful novels about the Far East sold millions of copies. *King Rat* (1962) became eligible for reversion in 2018 under the 56-year rule that governs pre-1978 works, while *Tai Pan* (1966) will not be eligible until 2021 and *Shogun* (1975) not until 2031. On the other hand, *Noble House* (1981) became eligible in 2016 under the 35-year rule governing post-1978 works, while *Whirlwind* (1986) and *Gai-Jin* (1993) will not be eligible until 2021 and 2028, respectively. The digital rights in all of these books, however, probably reverted to Clavell's heirs in 2002 after *Rosetta* was decided, assuming his book contracts were worded similarly to Vonnegut's.

Given his stature as a bestselling storyteller (Clavell also wrote the screenplays for *The Fly, The Great Escape,* and *To Sir with Love*), it's surprising that only five of Clavell's six books are currently in print in new paperback and Kindle editions sold by Random House, which is one of the top five publishers in the US (along with Macmillan, Simon & Schuster, Hachette, and HarperCollins). Astonishingly, Clavell's number-one bestseller, *Whirlwind* (1986), a tale of the Iranian revolution, is no longer in print in the US.

In its 1986 article on the publication of *Whirlwind,* the *New York Times* described Clavell as "the undisputed king of commercial fiction."[10] It reported that

Clavell auctioned off the rights to the book to William Morrow Publishing (now part of HarperCollins) for a then-record advance of $5 million, having allowed the bidders to read only the first 200 pages. Very few authors, then or now, have the market power to demand such advantageous terms. As I write this, 32 years after its publication, *Whirlwind* is the fifth-bestselling fiction book in the Middle Eastern category in the UK-Amazon Kindle store. However, UK-Amazon will not sell the book in any version to buyers outside of the UK.

So, why can UK readers download a Kindle version of *Whirlwind* or buy a new paperback edition, but US customers cannot? There's no reason the book would not sell in the US. UK readers give it more than four out of five stars, and Random House currently offers all five of Clavell's other books in the US.

But Random House, which might like to publish all of Clavell's works, does not own the US copyright in *Whirlwind*. HarperCollins does, and it chooses to keep the book out of print, perhaps because it owns only the US rights and does not want to invest any effort that won't reach Clavell's substantial world-wide market.

Why the *Rosetta* case has not produced a Kindle version of *Whirlwind* authorized by Clavell's heirs is a bit more mysterious. Here's a theory: a patent on an early e-reader was filed in 1985[11] and, by 1986, when *Whirlwind* was published, Morrow/HarperCollins may have written a contract that clearly forced him to sign away his digital rights. As noted above, *Rosetta* did not magically help all authors get rights to their e-books, just those authors with contracts similar to Vonnegut's 1960s–70s era agreements.

The reversion statutes seem to be the only hope for getting the book back in print in the US. In 2021, when Clavell's heirs are able to obtain the copyright in *Whirlwind* from HarperCollins, will they bring it back in print? If so, we would have a concrete example of the usefulness of the US reversion right.

With that question in mind, in 2017 I assembled three databases of book titles to assess the extent to which reversion might have a positive effect on the book market. First, I selected 60 authors who had two things in common with Clavell: (1) each had an end-of-year, top 10 *New York Times* bestseller, and (2) each published multiple books over a span of years, making some of their titles eligible for reversion but others not. I then generated a list of all 817 books (not all bestsellers) published by these authors.

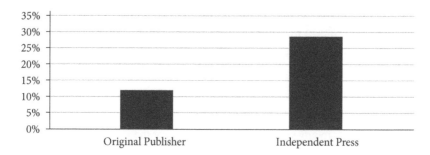

FIGURE 3.1. Reversion-Ineligible Books (248) by Type of Publisher: Percentage in Print in 2018. Source: Data from Paul J. Heald, "Copyright Reversion to Authors (and the Rosetta Effect): An Empirical Study of Reappearing Books," 66 Journal of the Copyright Office Society 59 (2019): 80.

Second, I gathered 692 books that appeared at least once in the top 10 weekly *New York Times* bestsellers lists from 1956 to 1986. And finally, to get a sample of some nonfiction and non-bestselling fiction, I randomly identified 454 books reviewed in the *New York Times* from 1978 to 1984. After inquiring into the publication histories of all 1,909 titles, I concluded that 20–23 percent of the books were in print in 2017 only because of reversion (including the *Rosetta* effect).

Oddly, the effect of reversion is the easiest to see in a sample of titles that are *ineligible* under the 35-year or 56-year termination rule. For example, in my sample of 817 books by bestselling authors, 248 of the titles, with a median publication date of 1967, were not eligible for either sort of statutory reversion. In theory, the original publisher retained control of the copyrights in all those titles. Of those, they kept 12 percent in print. The rest of the titles presumably fell outside of their business models. Interestingly, a whopping 29 percent of the same sample were kept in print by a variety of small and new independent presses (see fig. 3.1).

Why were so many of these books kept in print by independent publishers? Examining the websites of the small presses clarifies the situation. Open Road Media, for example, the most active of the independents, was founded in 2009 and specializes in publishing digital editions. Open Road is "committed to bring back the backlist, making reverted titles and works that have never been converted to digital format widely available as ebooks." It emphasizes that its "program is for authors whose rights have reverted." Smaller presses like Open

Road have more flexible business models than the "big five" US publishers and thus are able to fill a niche in the market with reverted titles.

Hold on! The sample described above is of reversion-*ineligible* books. How can reversion be at work there?

Figure 3.2 shows that 19 percent of the sample are in print only as e-books. These almost certainly represent digital rights freed up by the *Rosetta* case. Open Road Media and similar presses are happy to collaborate with authors or authors' heirs to take advantage of the exploitation of rights that *Rosetta* made possible. The original publisher is keeping bound volumes of these works out of print, so we can conclude that 19 percent of the sample is in print as stand-alone e-books because *Rosetta* freed up authors or their heirs to find alternative publishers for the works.

The 10 percent of the titles published by small independent presses in *bound* volumes (usually paperback) needs a bit more explaining because the original publishing houses should still own all rights in all of those editions. Here are two possible explanations.

First, some authors had enough bargaining power to negotiate contracts that reverted rights if the publisher took the book out of print. This would permit a deal to be struck later with a press like Open Road. In theory, a small press could also purchase rights from a larger publisher, but they are typically undercapitalized, and an exhaustive search of their business model descriptions contains no hint that independent presses buy rights from the big five publishers.

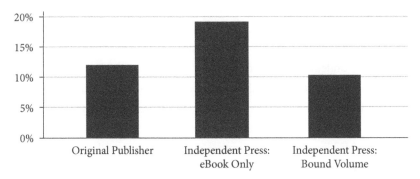

FIGURE 3.2. Reversion-Ineligible Books (248) by Type of Publisher: Percentage of eBooks and Bound Volumes in 2018. Source: Author (unpublished).

The second possibility is more likely and illustrates nicely the insight that won Richard Thaler the 2017 Noble Prize in Economics for his "Nudge" theory. To take advantage of either the 35-year or 56-year reversion statute, an author or her heirs must send a formal notice to the assignee of the copyright (almost always the original publisher). That notice letter can be sent up to 10 years prior to the earliest possible date that the original agreement can be terminated. This letter undoubtedly sometimes acts as a "nudge" to the publisher, which can respond to the notice in three ways: (1) "Hmm . . . we hadn't thought about this book for a while. Thanks for the prompt! Let's put out a new edition!" (2) "We can't be bothered with you now. You must wait until the statutory termination date." (3) "We have no interest in the book. Go ahead with your own publication whenever you like."

The third response best explains why 10 percent of the sample consists of bound volumes (with accompanying e-books) published by independent presses with no connection to the original publisher. Interestingly, the first response suggests that the reversion scheme might be responsible for some of the 12 percent of titles in print with the original publisher.

Another interesting observation is that the 521 reversion-eligible books by the same set of authors are in print at similar rates. The original publishers kept 13 percent in print, while independent presses, taking advantage of statutory reversion rules and *Rosetta*, kept 24 percent in print.

Figure 3.3 summarizes all 1,909 books from the three samples, including nonfiction books and non-bestsellers. The bar labeled "Independent Publisher" represents books that most likely appear in print due to rights reversion to authors. The 24 percent of 1,909 total books in the sample represents all books offered by independent publishers where the original publisher has ceased publishing the title. Most of those titles fell into two categories: (1) books eligible for reversion in 2017 under the 35-year or 56-year rule; and (2) so-called *Rosetta* books, stand-alone digital versions with no corresponding bound volumes.

Breaking down the categories of books, the original publishers do best with titles that are bestsellers, keeping more than 60 percent in print. Even so, independent publishers offer almost another 30 percent of bestsellers to consumers. Independent publishers far outshine their larger, better-established counterparts in the sample of books by bestselling authors, which included many

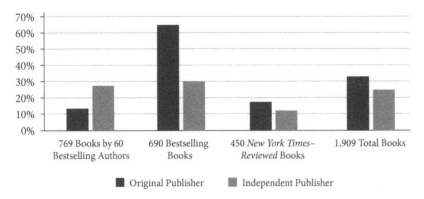

FIGURE 3.3. Percentage of To-Selling Books in Print in 2017: Original Publisher versus Independent Publisher. Source: Data from Paul J. Heald, "Copyright Reversion to Authors (and the Rosetta Effect): An Empirical Study of Reappearing Books," 66 Journal of the Copyright Office Society 59 (2019): 91.

non-bestselling titles. The independents, exploiting all three sorts of reversion, keep more than twice as many books (27 percent) in this sample in print as traditional publishers (13 percent). Not surprisingly, neither do particularly well with the category of books reviewed in the *New York Times* from 1978 to 1984, which contains mostly nonfiction and non-bestselling titles.

Although it looks like reversion has a positive effect, we should consider the possibility that a book might fall out of print after an author gets his rights back. Perhaps some authors or their heirs drop the ball after year 35, letting a title disappear. I checked a subsample of post-1978 publications for which I could determine the status of a title at year 30, five years before reversion. I looked to see whether a book in print in year 30 dropped out of print after year 35, and I found only one example out of 310 books: *The Best of Jazz* (1998) by Humphrey Lyttleton (1921–2008). An Englishman, Lyttleton was a jazz musician, BBC radio personality, cartoonist for the *Daily Mail*, and president of the Society for Italic Handwriting. A WWII veteran, Lyttleton landed on the shores of Italy during Operation Avalanche "with his pistol in one hand, and his trumpet in the other."[12]

Lyttleton would probably not approve of his heirs letting one of his books go out of print. But the estate is likely located in the UK, and perhaps his heirs can be forgiven for not knowing the rather murky US statutes governing rights reversion.

Murky or not, the rules seem to form a corner of copyright law that is doing a good bit of work in the public interest, helping to address the problem of the disappeared books of the twentieth century.

CHAPTER FOUR

REVENGE OF THE PORN PARODY

SO FAR, I HAVE NEGLECTED to discuss a key argument made in favor of a long, even infinite, copyright term—that famous works need owners to prevent misuse. In other words, Disney needs the eternal power to prohibit, for example, the production of a Mickey Mouse porn movie. Without this eternal power, the value of Mickey Mouse might be destroyed. The argument has a surface appeal, even to some economists. Don't copyright owners have strong incentives to prevent inappropriate uses from devaluing their assets?

Let's unpack this assertion. First of all, the most commonly voiced worry about misuse inevitably involves pornographic adaptations of famous works or depictions of famous characters. But remember, even if we strongly disapprove of Mickey, Minnie, and Goofy getting their freak on, we will never have to see the end product. Most porn cannot legally be shoved in our faces (at least, not if we're careful in our Internet searching). We generally have to seek it out, and no one can make us watch a movie of our favorite cartoon characters in flagrante.

Might not the mere knowledge of Disney porn lower our estimation of the iconic mouse and his friends? Well, to save you the trouble, in 2018, I paid a visit to the Internet Adult Film Database (iafd.com) to test this theory, using Santa Claus as an example. I stopped counting at 72 porn movies starring Santa or Mrs.

Claus, including the enchantingly titled *Santa's Twerkshop*. You can do your own searching, if you doubt me, and you'll find endless numbers of dirty films starring your favorite characters from childhood fiction. Even the Greek gods are not safe, as they frequently find themselves the subject of creative gay cinema. Has the longtime existence of these movies been ruining your Christmases? Do you now regret your college major was Greek mythology? Probably not.

But what about inappropriate uses of copyrighted works that we cannot avoid? What about the same tired song appearing in the background of commercials or in elevators or shopping malls? This speculation is still a poor argument for perpetual copyright. For one thing, radio stations, advertisers, and retailers have strong incentives not to annoy you with music or offensive images. Businesses have a natural incentive not to overuse or misuse your favorite songs or to offend you with pornography. Nonetheless, I'll admit to being tired of the famous thumping chorus from Carl Orff's cantata *Carmina Burana* (1935) being used in advertisements. But "O Fortuna" (the opening and closing movement) is actually a good counterexample. It's still under copyright, and its owner is supposedly protecting it from devaluing uses.

In fact, copyright owners do a pretty terrible job of preventing their works from being tarnished. Check out the various lists of the "worst movies made from books." Critics all have their own idea about what constitutes a terrible movie, but most of the films they savage (e.g., the film version of Frank Herbert's *Dune* (1984) with Sting commanding sci-fi versions of Tweedledum and Tweedledum to commit suicide) are made from books still under copyright.[1] The most scientific film website, *Metacritic*, lists 10 real stinkers based on its aggregation of numerous third-party movie reviews.[2] Only one of them, a live action remake of *Pinocchio*, derives from a public domain work. All 10 of MSN's list of the 10 worst movies made from children's books were made with the permission of the copyright holder.[3] If we believe that a bad movie devalues the book on which it is based, then copyright owners seem to do a poor job of stewardship.

Even when authors are good stewards of a work, do we necessarily want to give their heirs permanent control? A. A. Milne's son, resentful of his emotionally distant father, might have taken *Winnie-the-Pooh* out of print, or J. R. R. Tolkien's son might authorize a film version of *The Silmarillion* only if he, rather than Peter Jackson, directs the film. After a copyright expires, we might want the market to decide the fate of the work. We like competition in the market for pizza, so why not in the market for Mickey Mouse?

Your answer might depend on your response to a recent performance of the iconic Gershwin opera, *Porgy and Bess* (1934).[4] The Gershwin estate consistently requires that only black actors perform *Porgy and Bess*. (I don't use the term "African American" because the estate does not object to African singers or European performers of African descent.) However, a recent license to the Hungarian State Opera apparently failed to include the usual racial restriction. The opera company, employing a primarily Caucasian cast, sets the production in a Hungarian train station (or airport) and changes the ethnic focus to Middle Eastern migrants fleeing violence in their home countries.[5]

When *Porgy and Bess* falls into the public domain in 2029, we can expect even more radical departures from the Gershwin racial template. The question is not whether the Hungarian production is good or bad but whether the public benefits from having the chance to choose among multiple versions of the opera. After the copyright expires, some companies will produce the traditional version (at a lower cost since a license need not be obtained), while others will adapt it to fit their own purposes.[6] No member of the public will be forced to watch anything other than the traditional version, just as no one was forced to watch the Stalinist *Macbeth* with Patrick Stewart[7] or the nude, all-male production of *Hamlet*.[8]

And speaking of the nude, all-male production of *Hamlet*, does your new knowledge of that production reduce the value of the play to you?

Those who are upset by the liberties that producers and movie directors take with iconic works often have a deep respect for the author's original intent or have concerns for the author's feelings or those of her heirs. In some jurisdictions, especially France, the law recognizes an author's "moral" right to override expressive choices made by users of a work, even when that user is not violating copyright law. A recent French case involved the heirs of Victor Hugo suing the author of unauthorized sequels to *Les Miserables* (1862), a work long out of copyright. In the US, such a suit would be laughed out of court, but in France, the judge remanded the case for further consideration of the quality of the objectionable sequels. The most famous French moral rights judgment allowed the heirs of movie director John Huston to prevent the showing in France of an unauthorized colorized version of *The Asphalt Jungle* (1950). Huston's heirs did not own the copyright in the film, but they were allowed to assert their father's moral right to prevent the alteration of his creation.

The main reason US copyright law is generally unreceptive to moral rights claims (except in the context of some visual art works), is because weighing the interests at stake is well-nigh impossible. Think of *Porgy and Bess*. When its copyright expires in 2029, at least two positive things will happen: (1) producing the show will cost significantly less because producers will no longer have to buy a license (a clear economic benefit to the public); and (2) more radical variations of the opera will be produced (diversity also usually counts as a public benefit). On the negative side, (1) new versions might have a negative emotional impact on the Gershwin heirs and those who feel vicarious outrage for them; and (2) the work's cultural stability might be lost (its social meaning might evolve).

US judges are very uncomfortable balancing these four interests, so the law latches on to the most salient feature—how moving the work into the public domain lowers production costs. That's measurable. Of course, we could also measure with precision the heirs' loss of income, but that's not a public loss. In fact, that loss represents a gain to the public. "Moral" concerns generally fall by the wayside in US copyright law.[9]

So, how have concerns over the "tarnishment" of works nonetheless wormed their way into US law? A brief foray into trademark law, where the argument has greater life, is instructive (and trademark law brings us back to sex).

Here's a quote from a 2002 federal court of appeals case:

> Now suppose that the "restaurant" that adopts the name "Tiffany" is actually a striptease joint. . . . [C]onsumers will not think the striptease is under joint ownership with the jewelry store. But because of the inveterate tendency of the human mind to proceed by association, every time they think of the word "Tiffany" their image of the fancy jewelry store will be tarnished by the association of the word with the strip joint.[10]

In trademark law, the polluting of meaning has more traction, perhaps because the benefit to the public of allowing "inappropriate" uses of a trademark is more difficult to discern. Normally, proving trademark infringement requires proving that consumers are likely to be confused by an unauthorized use, but in the case cited above, associating a luxury trademark with a strip club was considered enough to constitute illegal trademark tarnishment.

Trademark tarnishment cases seem obsessed with the creation of sexual associations. In a case brought by the Victoria's Secret lingerie franchise, the Sixth Circuit Court of Appeals held that the law "create[s] a kind of rebuttable presumption, or at least a very strong inference, that a new mark used to sell sex-related products is likely to tarnish a famous mark if there is a clear semantic association between the two."

In discussing a small sex shop named Victor's Little Secret, the court reasoned that the association "between a famous mark and lewd or bawdy sexual activity disparages and defiles the famous mark and reduces the commercial value of its selling power." The court noted that it was making "an economic prediction about consumer taste and how the predicted reaction of conventional consumers in our culture will affect the economic value of the famous mark."[11] Of course, Victoria's Secret already trades in sexuality, so the court predicted that slightly naughty marks can be tarnished by still naughtier associations.

Here's a taste of some other court opinions:

1. *Pfizer Inc. v. Sachs* (2009).[12] Defendants' display at an adult entertainment exhibition of two models riding a VIAGRA-branded missile and distributing condoms would likely harm the reputation of Pfizer's trademark.

2. *Kraft Foods Holdings, Inc. v. Helm* (2002).[13] Pornographic website's use of "VelVeeda" tarnishes VELVEETA trademark.

3. *Mattel, Inc. v. Internet Dimensions Inc.* (2000).[14] Linking Barbie doll with pornography will adversely color the public's impressions of the doll.

4. *Polo Ralph Lauren L.P. v. Schuman* (1998).[15] Defendants' use of "The Polo Club" or "Polo Executive Retreat" as an adult entertainment club tarnished POLO trademark.

5. *Toys "R" Us, Inc. v. Akkaoui* (1996).[16] Toys "R" Us trademark was tarnished by the use of adultsrus.com as a domain name for a pornographic website.

6. *Hasbro, Inc. v. Internet Entm't Grp., Ltd.* (1996).[17] Adult entertainment website candyland.com put the reputation of the children's board game in grave danger.

7. *Pillsbury Co. v. Milky Way Prods., Inc.* (1981).[18] Defendant's sexually oriented variation of the Pillsbury Doughboy tarnished plaintiff's mark.

8. *Dallas Cowboys Cheerleaders, Inc. v. Pussycat Cinema, Ltd.* (1979).[19]

Pornographic depiction of a Dallas Cowboys cheerleader in an adult film tarnished the trademark of the Dallas Cowboys football team.

You get the idea.

Similar fears of tarnishment leak into copyright law in two ways. First, it's offered as a policy argument to extend copyright terms indefinitely. Economist William Landes and Judge Richard Posner, two of the strongest proponents of the tarnishment theory, suggest that "if anyone were free to incorporate the Mickey Mouse character in a book, movie, song, etc., the value of the character might plummet."[20] Therefore, they conclude, Disney should be able indefinitely to protect its copyrights.

Second, fears of tarnishment can affect a court's "fair use" analysis. In the 1970s, a group of satirists in California began producing *Air Pirates Funnies*, a cartoon magazine that targeted Mickey Mouse and his friends, turning them into dope-smoking, narcotics-trafficking, free-loving, and generally disreputable antiheroes. Disney was not amused.

Were the comic books, as claimed by their authors, a permissible fair use of Disney characters to criticize corporate greed and hypocrisy, or were they just a commercial rip-off?

Parody, Mickey, and Fair Use

The fair use test in the US requires judges to discuss and balance four factors: the nature of the use, the nature of the copied work, the amount taken, and the effect on the market for the copied work. Since the Supreme Court's discussion of parody in *Campbell v. Acuff-Rose Music* (1994), the "nature of the use" inquiry has favored unauthorized parodists.[21] *Campbell* concerned the rap group 2 Live Crew's parody of Roy Orbison's hit "Oh, Pretty Woman" (1964). The rap version contained some pretty nasty gender-shaming, hair-slamming lyrics set to the original song's famous thumping bass riff. Here's just a taste:

Bald headed woman you know your hair could look nice
Bald headed woman first you got to roll it with rice
Bald headed woman here, let me get this hunk of biz for ya
Ya know what I'm saying you look better than Rice-a-Roni[22]

The Court explained that parody is a time-honored, politically important category of speech worthy of protection, regardless of the knockoff's lame humor or questionable social commentary. If the first factor of the fair use test favored 2 Live Crew, then it's a good bet that it would favor the authors of *Air Pirates Funnies*.

The second factor, the nature of the copied work, should favor Disney. Mickey and his crew are creative artistic works. Courts don't accord much protection to fact-heavy works like history books, newspaper articles, encyclopedias, dictionaries, and phone books, but art works, like cartoons, are typically given the highest level of protection. Of course, to effectively parody a truly artistic work, someone needs to borrow quite a bit of the work, so most courts in parody cases find that the second factor doesn't carry too much weight.

Same for the third factor. A parodist has to copy enough of the artistic work for the audience to recognize what is being parodied, so courts generally deemphasize the third factor in parody cases. Nonetheless, *Campbell* suggests that it is possible to take too much. The *Air Pirates* cartoonists slavishly copied the Disney characters over hundreds of pages. Perhaps, they could have made their point just as well with less copying.

Given the mish-mash of the first three factors (no court has ever provided a mathematical balancing formula in fair use cases), the fourth factor is key: what is the effect of the parody on the market for the underlying work?

Those who take tarnishment theory seriously would assert that works like *Air Pirates Funnies* would severely compromise the market for the Disney characters. Audiences would mentally associate Mickey, Minnie, and Goofy with drugs, sexual misconduct, and violent crime instead of wholesome American values. The public might even purchase less Disney memorabilia or be less inclined to visit Disneyland or Disney World. And imagine if porn parodists got the green light to target Disney movies like *The Little Mermaid, Pocahontas, Mulan, Cinderella*, and *Sleeping Beauty*?

Tarnishment theory suggests that the fourth fair use factor, and therefore the entire fair use determination, should count against folks like the authors of *Air Pirate Funnies*.

The Court in *Campbell* addressed the issue of harm resulting from the parody of an artistic work. By analogy, Justice Souter recognized that trenchant criticism can negatively affect the market for a work, but the law tolerates that sort of damage (recall the devastating review of *By Love Possessed*). A cutting parody similarly can change people's attitudes toward a work. For example, the original (and unrealistically proportioned) Barbie doll (a copyrighted sculptural work by Mattel) was effectively parodied by the inventors of Trailer Trash Barbie and Biker Barbie. Barbie parodies meshed nicely with increasing feminist criticism of the doll in the press and on the radio, such as Aqua's 1997 hit *Barbie Girl*. Courts generally have allowed critical parodies of Barbie, despite the possibility that they will tarnish the Mattel brand.[23]

But what about *Air Pirates Funnies*? Did that parody go too far, or are all parodies legal fair uses? The original opinion condemning the comic was decided before *Campbell*, so it's fair to ask whether the case would come out the same way today.

The answer is unclear. First, *Air Pirates Funnies* takes as much of the Disney characters as possible. By comparison, 2 Live Crew took the bass riff of "Oh, Pretty Woman" and messed around with the melody, but it's not the same song. Aqua used the words "Barbie Girl" and mocked her valley girl lifestyle, but the album cover doesn't contain an image of a real Barbie doll. Even Trailer Trash Barbie (an actual doll, burstingly pregnant, buck-toothed, and smoking a cigarette) is clearly an original derivative work and not just a copy.

Second, the critical commentary made by *Air Pirates Funnies* is indirect, verging on satire rather than parody. The primary target seems more to be US drug laws and sexual hypocrisy in American culture and less Disney itself. In a post-*Campbell* case, the Ninth Circuit Court of Appeals thought this distinction mattered. It considered whether the book *The Cat NOT in the Hat,* illustrated in the style of Dr. Seuss and authored by "Dr. Juice," constituted a protected parody. The subject of the book was the infamous O. J. Simpson murder case, and the court found that appropriating the copyrighted Seuss works for the purpose of making a critical point about O.J. was not a fair use.[24]

Moving from Law to Facts

Applying tarnishment theory to fair use is messy, but some clarity might come from questioning the plausibility of the theory itself. If, as a matter of fact, sexual imagery does not tarnish, then the application of the theory becomes mostly moot. So far, lawyers have questioned whether a tarnishing satire should be a protected fair use in a factual vacuum. The debate has assumed, in the complete absence of empirical evidence, that tarnishment occurs, especially when the associations are sexual in nature. Given the role tarnishment theory has played in the term extension debate and its relevance in the fourth factor of the fair use analysis, the assumption of harm is worth interrogating.

So, Christopher Buccafusco (yes, his real name!) and I set out to tarnish some iconic works, to test the theory.

First, we went online and recruited more than a thousand subjects while pretending to be running a movie theater needing input on what movies to show. Our first group of subjects were shown pairs of movie posters for films that had come out in the same year. After receiving a one-sentence reminder of each movie's plot, participants advised us on which of the two to show in our "classic film series." For example, they were shown posters and descriptions of *Titanic* (1997) and *Good Will Hunting* (1997) side by side and asked which movie we should show. Other pairs included *You've Got Mail* (1998) and *Shakespeare in Love* (1998), and *Bourne Identity* (2002) and *Mission Impossible* (2002).

These subjects gave us a baseline level of the popularity of each film. For example, 35.2 percent preferred *Titanic* to *Good Will Hunting*, and 48.9 percent of the subjects preferred *You've Got Mail* to *Shakespeare in Love*.

Next, we tried to knock down those numbers by tarnishing the films. We gathered another thousand-plus group and tried to change their preferences by exposing them to posters for pornographic versions of 10 of the films. We did not show them actual porn films, but we did expose them to non-obscene images advertising porn versions of the films. This seemed a realistic test, given that members of the public often cannot control their encounters with posters but can control whether they see a film.

We told our second group of subjects that we wanted to schedule some spicy adult features for special late-night showings. "Could you help us choose between these two titles?" In this way, we tried to negatively influence the subjects' preferences for the original *Titanic* and *You've Got Mail* productions (see fig. 4.1). If tarnishment theory is correct, then associating the original films with pornography should create harmful impressions in consumers' minds.

To test whether preferences for *Titanic*, *You've Got Mail*, and other titles were diminished, we later presented the same subjects with our original classic movie pairs: *Titanic* and *Good Will Hunting*, *You've Got Mail* and *Shakespeare in Love*, and so on. Tarnishment theory would predict that the preference for *Titanic* and

FIGURE 4.1. Porn Parody Poster from Tarnishment Study. Source: Popsugar.com; Deathbyfilms.com.

You've Got Mail and other "tarnished" classics would move downward from the baseline levels established in our first survey.

Instead, the preference levels were positively affected by porn.

After being exposed to the *Bitanic* poster, subjects' preferences for *Titanic* rose from 35.2 percent to 42.9 percent. After being exposed to the *You Got She-Male* poster, subjects' preferences for *You've Got Mail* increased from 48.5 percent to 52.5 percent. Overall, porn parody posters were associated with a significant increase in the subjects' preferences for our 10 target movies as a group.

Such a study doesn't prove that tarnishment never happens, but it suggests that an alleged victim of tarnishment, either in the trademark or copyright context, should be required to put forth positive empirical evidence of market harm. A legal presumption that every association with sex harms a copyrighted (or trademarked) work seems unsupported, and the assertion that copyrights should last forever to prevent tarnishment seems utterly without foundation.

A Concluding Story about Audiobooks

Interestingly, in another experiment, coauthor Christopher Buccafusco (that *is* his real name) and I showed that tarnishment does sometimes happen.

We wanted to see whether audiobooks made from public domain novels were as good as those made from copyrighted novels. Why? Because enthusiasts of indefinite copyright terms assert that works need perpetual owners to make sure that they'll be used properly.[25] In particular, they claim that works need owners who, by nature of their monopoly right, have the maximum incentive to invest in the creation of new derivative versions of works. By this reasoning, a book still under copyright would make a higher-quality movie because the copyright owner would be motivated to carefully screen potential movie directors.[26] Similarly, audiobooks made from copyrighted novels would be better and more plentiful because their owners could grant an exclusive license and act as a steward, assuring high production values.

Theories are made to be tested, so we selected a group of public domain and copyrighted novels from roughly the same literary era and obtained audiobook versions of the works when possible. Among the copyrighted works were *Beau Geste* (1924) by P. C. Wren, *An American Tragedy* (1925) by Theodore Dreiser, *The Sound and the Fury* (1929) by William Faulkner, and *All Quiet on the Western Front* (1929) by Erich Maria Remarque. Among the public domain works were *O Pioneers!* (1913) by Willa Cather, *Portrait of the Artist as a Young Man* (1916) by James Joyce, *Age of Innocence* (1920) by Edith Wharton, and *Babbitt* (1922) by Sinclair Lewis. We asked subjects to listen to the first five minutes of the fifth chapter of each audiobook and to rate each reader. In theory, the owners of the copyrighted works should engage in quality control. Ownerless public domain works, lacking a steward, should have poorer-quality readers.

First, we asked one of our students, Alex, to record all the audiobook excerpts. We recruited subjects to listen to Alex's excerpts and rate the quality of his reading. (We also asked them substantive questions about each excerpt to make sure they actually listened!) The subjects rated Alex almost exactly the same whether he was reading from the copyrighted or public domain works. This reassured us that any differences we found among the commercial readers of the audiobooks would be driven by their skills and qualities, and not by the relative popularity of the underlying books or the content of each five-minute segment.

After our 400 subjects finished listening to the excerpts, we asked them to rate each reader and then assign a monetary value to each work. We pretended to be an audiobook company evaluating the talent of auditioning readers, and we claimed our experiment had left us with a bunch of bound volumes of each work. We asked:

"We will have many spare copies of this book when recording is concluded. How much should we sell the books for?" We wanted to see whether a bad audiobook reading would negatively affect the subjects' valuation of the book.

We found that the quality of the reading correlated positively with the value attached by the subject to the underlying work. In other words, unpopular readings tended to be associated with a lower valuation of the book being read. Perhaps this is not surprising. Imagine a terrible movie version of a book. Might the movie negatively affect the chance the audience will purchase and read the book afterward?

Although not every bad reading resulted in a low valuation of the book, some examples of the overall trend are illustrative. On a five-point scale, the two worst readers of the copyrighted books scored 3.23 (*Arrowsmith*) and 3.62 (*Bridge over San Luis Rey*). Those books were valued by the listeners at $7.31 and $7.43, respectively. The more highly rated readers of *A Farewell to Arms* (4.44) and *Look Homeward, Angel* (4.55) scored much better, and the listeners valued those works at $10.83 and $9.35, respectively.

Among the public domain titles, the two worst readers scored 3.52 and 3.71 (*Of Human Bondage* and *The Beautiful and the Damned*), and the listeners valued those books at $7.48 and $7.59. The two best readers scored 4.9 and 4.75 (*Captain Blood* and *The Age of Innocence*), and the listeners valued those books at $9.45 and $11.

So, we can hardly take the position that tarnishment never occurs. Negative associations with works can affect value. Despite some inconsistencies in the data, the overall trend demonstrated that the valuation of the bound book correlated with the quality of its audio performance.

Perpetuating copyright ownership of book titles, however, is not the answer to improving the quality of audiobook readers. The study showed that books with owners were just as subject to tarnishment as books without owners. The copyright owners did no better job of choosing readers than did the open competitive market for ownerless public domain titles.

And perhaps this is not a surprise. If you were planning on recording and selling an audiobook of a public domain title like *Tarzan of the Apes* (1912), wouldn't you want to maximize your profits by choosing a good reader?

And think twice before making a porn version of *Tarzan* ... there are at least eight of them out there already.

CHAPTER FIVE

YOUTUBE

More Parody and Millions of Silent Bargains

COPYRIGHT LAW DOES NOT LOOK the same all over the world. For example, until recently there was no parody defense to copyright infringement under the law of the UK. The land of Monty Python, Rowan Atkinson, Ricky Gervais, and Peter Sellers frowned on 2 Live Crew lampooning "Oh, Pretty Woman" within its borders! The law of the European Union (EU) permitted member states to allow otherwise infringing parodies in 2001,[1] but the UK did not make an exception until 2014.[2] *Air Pirates Funnies* would definitely never have seen the light of day in the UK before the change.

One influential study that helped pave the way for the change in UK law also enhances our understanding of how unauthorized—and even objectionable—uses can live harmoniously with a copyrighted work.[3] The data also open our eyes to the life of copyrighted works on YouTube, which constitutes the boldest experiment yet in tolerated infringement, one that goes far beyond the acceptance of unauthorized parody.

Three innovative UK researchers led by Kris Erickson identified 375 songs that cracked the top 100 singles chart in the UK during 2011. They found an astounding average of 24 unauthorized YouTube video parodies per song, and they categorized the parodies as (1) Target Parodies (35 percent poked fun at or criticized the original song or performer), (2) Weapon Parodies (31 percent used the song to poke fun at or criticize another person or phenomenon unrelated to the original song), or (3) Self-Parodies (22 percent commented primarily on the parodists themselves). The remaining percentage of the videos were mash-ups or karaoke mislabeled as parodies.

Erickson's team also identified the official YouTube version of 343 of the original songs (32 of the initial 375 had no official authorized videos) and tracked the number of views each original authorized video earned over the same time period as its parodies. As figure 5.1 shows, the number of views of the original song increases with the number of parodies. The study concludes that "the presence of parody is positively correlated with size of audience for commercial music videos [and] the positive impact of parody is most significant for works that are not commercially successful before appearing on YouTube. These 'minor hits' appear to be most susceptible to a lift provided by publicity and awareness generated by a large number of parody videos available elsewhere on the platform."[4]

The study is not perfect. The original songs might have earned even more views in the absence of the parodies, but it seems evident that parodies don't destroy the market for the original. In fact, only 1.5 percent of the parodies studied actively discouraged the viewer from consuming the original. Moreover, the study found that parodists exhibited a high degree of creativity, with 49.6 percent writing new lyrics, 13.1 percent composing a new sound recording, and 86.3 percent filming a new video.

For these reasons, Erickson and his team concluded that the market for parody and the market for the original were two separate markets, satisfying two separate tastes (but not two completely separate sets of viewers, given that some people—like me—enjoying watching both the original and the parody). Importantly, the parodies were popular enough to generate commercial interest and significant advertising revenue without substituting for the original. This makes sense in light of the finding that parodists label their works as "parody" and often appear in their own videos, making clear they are offering a distinct product.

And here's another critical point: the valuable new parody product cannot effectively be offered by the original songwriter or producer. Consider the hilarious parody of Adele's "Hello" by Key of Awesome.[5] I love Adele, and she is a multitalented individual, but there's no way for her to compete with the Key of Awesome in pointing out the silliness of the official video and the predictability of the song. Adele's goal is to make us cry; the goal of the parody is to make us

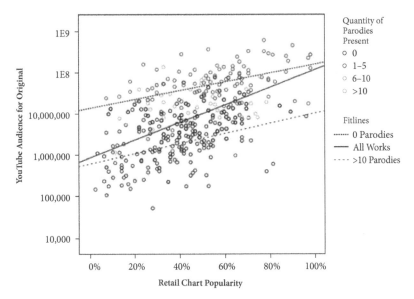

FIGURE 5.1.   Distribution of 343 Original Works and the Presence of Parodies.
Source: Kris Erickson et al., "Copyright and the Economic Effects of Parody: An
Empirical Study of Music Videos on the YouTube Platform and an Assessment of the
Regulatory Options," 20. https://www.gov.uk/government/uploads/system/uploads/at
tachmentdata/file/309903/ipresearch-parody-report3-150313.pdf.

laugh at how seriously she takes herself. Adele is famous for the agonized bar-
ing of her soul, for singing her way through a painful breakup. Key of Awesome
can target the ex-boyfriend in a more direct way: "I gave you an atomic wedgie
and I hope your crotch healed."

The public wants to watch Key of Awesome make a parody of "Hello," not
Adele. In other words, satisfying consumers in some commercial markets requires
unauthorized borrowing and the creation of derivative works by third parties.

This insight may further explain porn parodies. Even if Disney wanted to, it
would be financially irresponsible for it to satisfy the market for Mickey Mouse
porn. Imagine the boycotts of the Magic Kingdom! The reputational damage
to Disney would be massive. However, if an unauthorized parodist, over the
protest of Disney, animates *Mickey and Minnie's Vegas Hot Tub Adventure*, the
niche market for cartoon porn is satisfied without reputational damage to an
apoplectic Disney.

What's Special about YouTube

The Erickson parody study did not emphasize an important fact: at the time the parodies were created and uploaded, they were probably infringing in the UK, which lacked a parody exception at the time. Given that the copyright owners had the law on their side, why did they not demand the parodies be taken down?

The short answer is that copyright owners can benefit financially from infringement, and a close analysis of YouTube helps to explain why and how.

YouTube's highly automated system called Content ID quickly reports the upload of infringing music to owners. Content ID invites music copyright holders to submit digital files of their protected works to YouTube. The files act as digital fingerprints, allowing YouTube to identify unauthorized uploads as soon as they happen, even when the infringing music is just playing in the background of the video. If someone uploads a teary-eyed, breakup slide show on YouTube with Adele singing "Hello" in the background, YouTube will flag the homemade video on behalf of Universal Music (which owns the copyright in the written musical composition) and Sony Music Entertainment (which owns the copyright in the sound recording of the song).

This is a good opportunity to explain that a music video often has three copyright owners: (1) the owner of the copyright in the *composition*—the sheet music as written by the songwriter; (2) the owner of the copyright in the *sound recording*, usually the music studio that hired the sound engineers who created the mp3 file (or analog vinyl album); and (3) the owner of the copyright in the *video*—the moving images captured by the videographer. YouTube requires that anyone desiring to upload a video have permission to use all three copyrights.

Note that unless the performer of the song wrote it or recorded it himself, he has no copyright to assert!

We should ask one question before proceeding further: why is YouTube not instantly liable for copyright infringement when someone uploads an infringing video, especially since some estimates find that more than 90 percent of music uploaded to YouTube is unauthorized?

First of all, YouTube cannot be liable as a direct infringer because it merely provides the mechanism used by the infringing uploader of a song. What if someone borrows your phone and takes a picture of a copyrighted painting without your knowledge? Surely, you should not be liable. Direct liability requires that you actually take the photo yourself. Nonetheless, you might be *secondarily* liable for your friend's infringement if you knew beforehand that your friend was going to infringe: "Hey, can I borrow your camera to take this photo of a famous copyrighted artwork and sell posters of it?" In such a situation, you are (and should be) secondarily liable for your friend's primary action.

What about YouTube? It provides a mechanism whereby infringers can upload all sorts of infringing stuff. However, it is not directly liable when it merely provides the physical means. What about secondary liability for YouTube, which surely knows that some of its users upload unauthorized music? Under copyright law, general knowledge that people will misuse the service is not enough to make YouTube liable. In the absence of Content ID software, YouTube would not know whether any particular upload was infringing, but once it has specific knowledge, formally obtained through a notification from the copyright owner, it has a legal obligation to take down the infringing upload.

The Digital Millennium Copyright Act establishes this "notice and takedown" regime and provides YouTube with a safe harbor until it has actual knowledge of an infringement.[6] The law results in YouTube processing millions of takedown requests a month to avoid liability.

So, why did YouTube establish the Content ID program? In its absence, YouTube could more easily claim that it lacked specific knowledge of any particular illegal upload. Once it created the program, it could no longer deny knowledge of most music copyright infringement. First, if its music fingerprinting software program was reasonably easy to write and implement, then it may have had a legal obligation to develop it. Cases suggest strongly that "willful blindness" is as bad as actual knowledge. Second, the music lobby is strong in Washington, and YouTube was clever to implement Content ID as a concession to the lobby. Third, as we will see in a moment, all parties—illegal uploaders, consumers, copyright holders, and YouTube itself—benefit financially from the Content ID program.

To examine this claim, I created in May 2013 a dataset of popular songs and identified the uploader, the date and type of upload, the number of views, and whether the upload had been monetized through the addition of an advertisement.[7] I searched YouTube for the number-one song for each year from 1930 through 1970, in the US, France, and Brazil, and then studied the first 10 search results for each song. The US songs included "Over the Rainbow" (Judy Garland, 1939), "Que Será, Será" (Doris Day, 1956), and "Let's Twist Again" (Chubby Checker, 1961) (see table 5.1). Notable French songs from the same era included "Mon Legionnaire" (Edith Piaf, 1937), "Lily Marlene" (Marlene Dietrich, 1942), "La Vie en Rose" (Edith Piaf, 1946); Brazil's included "Tico no Fuba" (Oscar Aleman, 1932) and "Copacabana" (Carmen Miranda, 1947).

One striking statistic revealed that more than 95 percent of the videos appeared to have been uploaded by someone other than the copyright owner. Although it is impossible to tell whether "wehavejoy," an uploader who posted a

TABLE 5.1. Number of YouTube Listeners and Percentage of Retail Chart Popularity of Number-One Songs in the US.

US NUMBER-ONE SONG	YEAR
"Puttin' on the Ritz"	1930
"Minnie the Moocher"	1931
"Night and Day"	1932
"Stormy Weather"	1933
"Moon Glow"	1934
"Cheek to Cheek"	1935
"Pennies from Heaven"	1936
"Sing, Sing, Sing (With a Swing)"	1937
"Begin the Beguine"	1938
"Over the Rainbow"	1939
"In the Mood"	1940
"Chattanooga Choo Choo"	1941
"White Christmas"	1942
"Pistol Packin' Mama"	1943
"Swingin' on a Star"	1944
"Rum and Coca-Cola"	1945
"Prisoner of Love"	1946
"Chi-Baba, Chi-Baba"	1947
"Buttons and Bows"	1948

US NUMBER-ONE SONG (CONT.)	YEAR (CONT.)
"Ghost Riders in the Sky"	1949
"Third Man Theme"	1950
"Too Young"	1951
"You Belong to Me"	1952
"Vaya con Dios"	1953
"Mr. Sandman"	1954
"Rock around the Clock"	1955
"Que Será, Será"	1956
"Jailhouse Rock"	1957
"Tom Dooley"	1958
"Marina"	1959
"Are You Lonesome Tonight?"	1960
"Let's Twist Again"	1961
"If I Had a Hammer"	1963
"Strangers in the Night"	1966
"Whiter Shade of Pale"	1967
"Hey Jude"	1968
"Get Back"	1969

Source: Paul J. Heald, "How Notice-and-Takedown Regimes Create Markets for Music on YouTube: An Empirical Study," *UMKC Law Review* 83 (2014): 327–28.

video of Bill Haley's "Rock around the Clock," is unauthorized, a click on other videos posted by "wehavejoy" reveals a likely amateur who also uploaded a video of his or her cute Yorkshire Terrier named Molly. Only a handful of uploaders of hit music from this era seem to be the copyright owners. Those who appear to be owners, like "The Ed Sullivan Show" or "BingCrosbyVevo," use names that associate themselves with the legal owners of the material.

Most of the 95 percent of unauthorized uploads could have been taken down at the request of the copyright owner. Why weren't they? The answer lies in the electronic communication copyright owners have with YouTube when

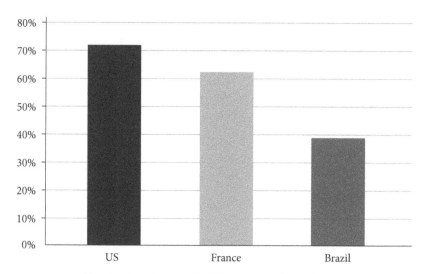

FIGURE 5.2. Number-One Songs in the US, France, and Brazil, 1930–60: Percentage of 300 Uploads Monetized. Source: Heald, "How Notice-and-Takedown Regimes Create Markets," 314.

an infringing song is discovered. A copyright owner has three choices: (1) tell YouTube to take down the video, (2) tolerate the infringement, or (3) leave the video up and make money through YouTube's advertising program. The third choice benefits the uploader, who successfully provides others access to a favorite work, as well as both the copyright owner and YouTube, who profit from the advertising revenue.

The first (take it down!) and third (gimme money!) choices are easy to understand. Tolerated infringement in the absence of advertising is the most puzzling category. Figure 5.2 shows that 73 percent of uploads of US number one songs from 1930–60 had been monetized. A little over 60 percent of French copyright owners, and a little under 40 percent of Brazilian copyright owners, placed ads.

Most striking, however, is how many illegal uploads were tolerated by the copyright owners but not monetized. Even US copyright owners, known for their vigilance, allowed 27 percent of the unauthorized uploads to be presented without ads. Furthermore, the timing of the uploads doesn't explain the failure to monetize. On average, the tolerated uploads had been on YouTube for four years at the time of the study—plenty of time for the copyright owners to discover them.

We can make several guesses as to why so much infringement is tolerated without being monetized. First, some of the French and Brazilian copyright owners may not be taking advantage of Content ID, perhaps because the songs have a small audience (see fig. 5.3). The French and Brazilian copyright owners were not leaving much money on the table. Why not let consumers enjoy the song without interruption in the hope of rebuilding an audience?

In addition, song owners from all countries, including the US, may be happy to have their tunes heard on YouTube without annoying listeners with advertisements. Although I have no access to revenue data, owners have an idea whether YouTube helps or hurts. If the average yearly revenue earned from a 1937 song in the pre-YouTube era is less than in the post-YouTube era, a composer (or more likely the publisher who owns the copyright) might be quite willing to tolerate unauthorized uploads. In fact, to the extent a copyright owner sees an increase in interest in a song or an uptick in sheet music sales, it may be silently applauding the uploader.

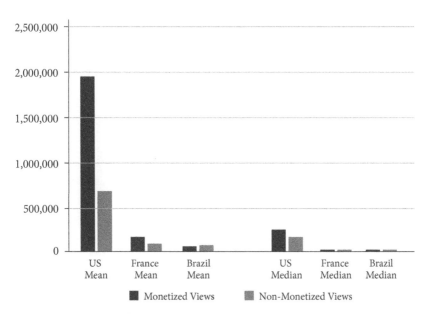

FIGURE 5.3.   Views of Number-One Songs in the US, France, and Brazil, 1930-60.
Source: Heald, "How Notice-and-Takedown Regimes Create Markets," 320.

In addition, the nature of the uploads may help explain the large amount of tolerated infringement. Figure 5.4 divides music uploads into four categories. A "custom video" consists of the recorded song being played in the background of a video made by an uploader, often a slide show (imagine Eric Clapton's "Tears in Heaven" playing over a funereal slide show). An "amateur performance" depicts the uploader or a friend singing the song without permission. A "recording" is the recorded song playing with a still photo, often an image of the album cover or old vinyl disk. A "TV or movie clip" usually contains the song as performed on a television program or in an excerpted film scene.

American copyright owners are not very tolerant of custom videos. Only about 8 percent of the nonmonetized uploads were weepy (or loving, or birthday, or travel—you get the idea) slide shows. US copyright owners were equally intolerant of amateur performances (although 30 percent of nonmonetized French uploads were folks singing their favorite French classics). Not surprisingly, few uploads (less than 20 percent in each country) consisted of nonmonetized music that was an identical copy of the recording and might substitute for the original song. The interesting question, of course, is why any such uploads are tolerated, rather than being taken down or monetized.

Comparing the pattern of nonmonetized uploads to monetized uploads is interesting (see fig. 5.5). Owners of US works focus on monetizing recordings.

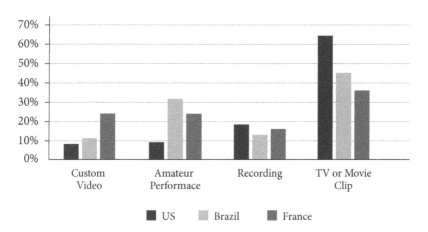

FIGURE 5.4. Percentage of Tolerated Infringement by Type of Upload. Source: Heald, "How Notice-and-Takedown Regimes Create Markets," 322.

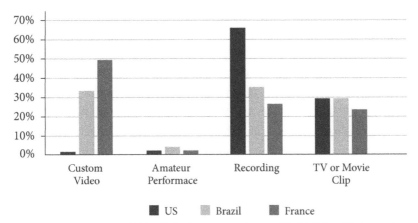

FIGURE 5.5. Monetized Uploads by Percentage. Source: Heald, "How Notice-and-Takedown Regimes Create Markets," 321.

As long as the upload is a perfect copy of the song, untainted by custom slides or video, many owners decide to run ads rather take it down. French and Brazilian copyright owners are far more interested than their US counterparts in monetizing custom videos. If the song playing in the background of a video is a perfect copy of the original, the foreign owners seem content to make a bit of a profit. No owners seem enthusiastic about monetizing amateur performances. Perhaps they are worried about tarnishment—a bad performance tainting the public impression of a song.

The most interesting data involve performances in television and movie clips (but mostly television). No group of copyright owners monetizes more than 30 percent of such uploads. One would think these would be the most frequently monetized (or the least frequently tolerated), given that three copyrights are potentially implicated in each upload. In a lip-synched performance (very common in old TV variety shows), the copyright in the music composition, in the recording, and in the moving images may all be infringed. In a live TV performance, the composition and the video copyrights are potentially infringed.

One explanation lies in the YouTube requirement that the party seeking to monetize an upload must own or have permission to exercise *all* relevant copyrights.[8] In other words, the owner of the copyright in the music *and* the owner of the copyright in the video must cooperate. The history of videotaping during the era when the sample songs were popular illustrates why cooperation is difficult to achieve. Yep, it's an orphan works issue.

Imagine the owner of the copyright in "Marieke" being notified by Content ID that "alenaapril" has uploaded a live performance of Jacques Brel singing the song. The owner visits the offending page and sees the image shown in figure 5.6. When did the performance occur? Which French (or Belgian or Dutch or German or US or UK) television channel broadcast the performance? At the time of the recording, was there an agreement assigning the copyright in the performance? Did the television station even record the performance? It is entirely possible that 50 years ago the song was recorded by a Brel fan pointing her 8mm movie camera at a television set while the station did not bother to record at all.

These questions are illuminated by knowledge of the practice, common until the early 1970s, of taping over live broadcasts! The television station that originally owned the copyright in the Brel performance (if it bothered to record at all) probably has no copy of the performance, nor any idea that it owns the copyright. A fascinating Wikipedia page is devoted to "lost" television broadcasts that were never recorded by the broadcaster or were recorded over and have not been found in private collections.[9] Most stunningly, the only copy of the first Superbowl is in private hands. NBC and CBS, who simulcast the game, both taped over it.[10] In a parallel tragedy for Europeans, the first Eurovision song contest was never recorded, and no bootleg copies are known to exist.

Indeed, bootleggers are responsible for preserving much of what survives of broadcast television from the 1940s through the 1960s. Even so, the list of missing American television is impressive: *The Ed Sullivan Show* episode marking Jerry Lewis's and Dean Martin's initial TV appearance; 175 television shows produced by the DuMont Television Network whose shows included the first sitcom, the first soap opera, *Ted Mack's Original Amateur Hour*, and Jackie Gleason's *Cavalcade of Stars*; the color version of Rodgers and Hammerstein's *Cinderella* starring Julie Andrews; 10 years of *The Tonight Show*; and 97 episodes of *Dr. Who*, among many more.[11]

Given this state of affairs, one can understand the hopeless task facing the owner of the copyright in the song "Marieke." Getting the cooperation of the owner of the broadcast, as required by YouTube, is virtually impossible and probably not worth the effort, given the small amount of potential advertising earnings at stake.

FIGURE 5.6. Jacques Brel. Source: Screenshot from YouTube.

Unless the song's owner lies and claims it owns the video broadcast, the upload will go unmonetized, which explains why so few such uploads have ads.

The owner of "Marieke," of course, could take down the video. It is technically the victim of infringement. But why do it? It's free promotion for the song and for the artist, and it may help grow a new audience for one of the greatest singers of the twentieth century. No wonder that a whopping 64 percent of nonmonetized uploads of US number hits from 1930 to 1960 consist of television or movie clips.

Bootleggers and infringers who upload videos unlock our cultural past and undo some of the damage done by the short-sighted broadcasters who destroyed their own recordings (actress Edie Adams testified that three truckloads of the DuMont Network archive were unceremoniously dumped into the ocean).[12]

Most important, what makes the reappearance of these recordings possible is Content ID, in conjunction with the notice and takedown rules of the Digital Millenium Copyright Act. A typical uploader has no way to find the owner of a broadcast performance or to communicate directly with the owner of a music copyright. The uploader, however, can go ahead and post the material on You-Tube. YouTube will facilitate the availability of the performance without fear of its own liability. It need act only if it receives a takedown notice from the owner of the music copyright. As we now know, many owners of music copyrights will allow the upload to stay.

Notice how YouTube acts as an intermediary, reducing the cost of communication between two disparate parties. The uploader essentially proposes a transaction: "I want my friends to hear this song. Please leave it up—maybe you can make some money from it." The owner of the music copyright then responds by monetizing, taking down, or leaving it up without ads. Best of all, Content ID is highly automated. Thousands of these transactions are proposed and consummated every day, often through the operation of programmed software.

To use a fancy economic term, YouTube's Content ID system greatly lowers "transaction costs," much to the benefit of Jacques Brel fans everywhere and almost certainly to the benefit of the copyright owners of his songs.

CHAPTER SIX

BACH'S COPYRIGHT OR COPYFRAUD?

MY WIFE DIRECTS A CHOIR, which I began singing in during the early 1990s, and I started teaching copyright law at the University of Georgia about the same time. One Thursday night, she handed out a Johannes Brahms motet for us to sing. I was stunned, and not just because the piece was written for four-part women's voices. Much more disturbing, the sheet music for "*O Bone Jesu*," written in 1859,[1] bore the following warning at the bottom of the first page: "©Copyright 1979." Since Brahms died in 1897, I was baffled that the German music publisher Carus-Verlag claimed ownership of the piece. Surely the work was firmly in the public domain!

Thereafter, I began paying closer attention to the compositions residing in my music folder and the literary works in my library. I discovered that major publishers frequently pretended the public domain did not exist. I found, among hundreds, a J. S. Bach (1685–1750) concerto "copyrighted" in 2014,[2] a facsimile edition of Adam Smith's (1723–90) *Wealth of Nations* bearing a copyright date of 2006,[3] a William Billings (1746–1800) anthem ("Jordan") with a copyright date of 1954,[4] and a copy of the Declaration of Independence (1776) that carried a claim of "©Copyright 1956."[5]

Were publishers just being sloppy? Or was there something else going on?

A Bach cantata provided a hint. It contained a warning printed in grayscale to deter copiers: "COPYING IS ILLEGAL." By this point in the book, you know that this simplistic statement is not true (if you don't, please go back to page 1 and start over). The law says that it is perfectly permissible to copy works that are in the public domain. Indeed, one of the reasons we incentivize authors with copyright in the first place is to generate a large and vibrant public domain. At the bottom of the cantata was the proclamation that the publisher was the sole selling agent of the piece. Choir directors considering photocopying the work for distribution to their choirs will be deterred from doing so by the warning. Who wants to hand performers music that looks illegal?

So, instead of photocopying the piece at a cost of roughly three cents per page, most musicians will pay the dollar per page—or more—charged by the copyright claimant. In a private conversation, a Sony Music executive once told me that making copyright claims to public domain music was one of the oldest scams in the industry.

Numerous editions of public domain works state that you should send the Copyright Clearance Center in Washington, D.C., one dollar for each page that you photocopy. If you are bold, you could ignore the copyright symbol at the bottom of the page, but if you are a bit risk-averse, you may pay the requested fee, especially if you learn the potential consequences of being wrong. The civil penalties for a single act of deliberate copyright infringement top out at $150,000, and some purposeful, for-profit infringements qualify as crimes.

I will not insult your intelligence by spelling out the motivation of publishers who claim to own public domain materials to intimidate potential copiers.

My colleague, Jason Mazzone, catalogs abusive claims made by publishers in his *Copyfraud and Other Abuses of Intellectual Property Law*.[6] He describes copyright claims made to reprints of works by Charles Dickens (1812–70), Jane Austen (1775–1817), and Benjamin Franklin (1706–90); copies of *The Federalist Papers* (1788), the Constitution (1789), and the Declaration of Independence (1776); and greeting cards bearing images of Claude Monet's water lilies, Vincent van Gogh's sunflowers, and Paul Cézanne's apples. He notes that musical examples are especially prevalent, including "Beethoven's piano concertos, Chopin's nocturnes, Bach's cantatas, Handel's Messiah, or 'The Star Spangled Banner.'"

Mazzone offers a further example illustrating the abuse of the statute that puts all US government works in the public domain. For example, judicial opinion, statutes, and regulations are dedicated to the public domain from the time of their creation, as well as reports written by federal employees or photographs taken by them in the course of their duties. Mazzone describes Barnes and Noble's edition of the 1964 *Warren Commission Report* on the assassination of President John F. Kennedy. Although it is in the public domain, free to copy, the edition states that "[n]o part of this book may be used or reproduced in any manner whatsoever without written permission of the Publisher." This is a blatant lie.

To be sure, if Barnes and Nobles were to add a new introduction to the *Warren Commission Report* or insert new critical commentary, it could claim copyright on its own original incremental contribution, but no amount of new material can turn the public government report itself into a private document. Mazzone identifies an even more egregious example: a vendor that stated copying the *9/11 Commission Report* from its website would result in huge civil fines or prison time! Few would dare copy the public domain report without permission in the face of that bald-faced lie.

The Role of Originality

Many publishers, especially those in the music industry, make minor changes to scores to justify their copyright notices, implicitly claiming that the tweaking creates an independently protectable new work. As a matter of law, it is possible to derive a new work from an older one. Disney, for example, has made movies like *Snow White*, *Cinderella*, or *Pocahontas* based on public domain materials. Clearly, Disney writers, animators, and composers add sufficient value to render the movies independently copyrighted works. You cannot copy a Disney movie just because the story has a basis in the public domain.

To give a musical example, in his famous suite, *Appalachian Spring*, American composer Aaron Copeland imbeds an old Shaker folk tune, *Simple Gifts*, ("'tis a gift to be simple, 'tis a gift to be free ... ") to create a memorable dance-like moment. Copeland, of course, was borrowing folk music in the tradition of Frédéric Chopin, Edvard Grieg, and Béla Bartók, who found frequent inspiration in the folk tunes of their homelands (as Bach did before them, and medieval troubadours before him—you get the idea). Public domain sources have frequently been the building blocks of creative and original music. Give a quick listen to what the Electric Light Orchestra does to Ludwig van Beethoven's *Fifth Symphony*[7] or consider the folk-rap craze that swept Serbia in 2018.[8]

A composer can definitely change a piece of public domain music sufficiently to create a new work that is entitled to copyright protection. Not all contributions, however, are significant enough. Two prominent copyright experts, William Krasilovsky and Sidney Shemel, warn that "[m]uch of the music material in the public domain is tainted by vague and indefinite claims of copyright in minimal or obscure 'new versions.'"[9]

What sort of "new versions" are protected by copyright, and what sort of "new versions" are merely minimal changes designed to perpetrate a fraud on the public?

The Second Circuit Court of Appeals has considered the question on several occasions, including one interesting case involving an "Uncle Sam" bank, a toy that has its roots in nineteenth-century Americana.[10] Just put your coin in Uncle Sam's greedy little hand, pull a lever, and your money will clink down into the hollow pedestal through his bag (see fig. 6.1). The various versions of the cast-iron Uncle Sam bank, which were once protected sculptural works, fell into the public domain long ago through the expiration of their copyright terms.

In *L. Baitlin & Son v. Snyder*, the appellate court considered whether a more recent version of the bank, made out of plastic with some other minor alterations from its public domain predecessor, was sufficiently original to merit protection. A competitor of the plaintiff had slavishly copied the updated version of the bank instead of copying directly from the original public domain source. The court not only rejected the copyright claim, finding the plaintiff's updated bank insufficiently original, it issued a warning to others who would dare attempt to privatize a corner of the public domain by making minor changes to it:

> Absent a genuine difference between the underlying work of art and the copy of it for which protection is sought, the public interest in promoting progress in the arts—indeed, the constitutional demand . . . could hardly be served. To extend copyright-ability to minuscule variations would simply put a weapon for harassment in the hands of mischievous copiers intent on appropriating and monopolizing public-domain work.[11]

FIGURE 6.1. Uncle Sam Bank. Source: Wikimedia Commons.

The requirement of sufficient originality ("the constitutional demand") forms the bulwark protecting the public from the "weapon of harassment" that the copyright symbol can become. The public domain belongs to the public, and woe betide the seller who tries to lock out its competitors and, therefore, the public by making minor changes and claiming copyright.

Whether a work is sufficiently original (Copeland's *Appalachian Spring*) or not (Snyder's version of the Uncle Sam bank) can be a difficult line to draw, but courts have done a pretty good job of illustrating where it is.

In *Woods v. Bourne*, the Second Circuit considered whether several versions of the classic Tin Pan Alley hit "When the Red, Red, Robin goes Bob, Bob, Bobbin' Along" were sufficiently original.[12] In 1926, Harry Woods brought a "lead sheet," consisting of the song's lyrics and melody, to the predecessors (Irving Berlin, Inc.) of Bourne Music. Interestingly, Woods was born without any fingers on his left hand,[13] so he may have had less than the typical musician's interest in providing harmonies that might accompany the melody and lyrics (although Billboard Music once reported that he played a "terrific bass"[14]). Despite his disability, Woods was drafted into the army in WWI—demonstrating just how committed President Wilson was to defeating the Germans—and cultivated his interest in songwriting during his service. Afterward, he moved to New York City and soon became a very successful songwriter.

In any event, after the publisher decided to buy Woods's song, its in-house "technicians" provided a harmony and probably made some other adjustments to the original version of "Red, Red, Robin." A later arrangement substituted a moving bass line for the first technicians' quarter-note emphasis on the first and third beats in each measure. The court noted that the technicians had definitely made changes to Woods's composition. Certainly, the addition of the bass line made the song sound somewhat different. The court, however, refused to find that the two subsequent versions of Woods's song were sufficiently original to constitute separate protected derivative works.

In the lower court opinion, the district court tellingly described the additional harmonies as "conventional" and then found that a new arrangement of preexisting composition must contain "more than mere 'cocktail pianist variations' . . . something of substance [must be] added making the piece to some extent a new work with the old song embedded in it."[15] This reflects the sensibilities of an older opinion from Georgia that considered whether adding an alto line to public domain compositions in *The Sacred Harp* hymnal constituted a change sufficient enough to merit protection. As you can see in figure 6.2, the original version of "Amazing Grace" ("New Britain" is the name of the tune), one of the most famous pieces in *The Sacred Harp*, has only three lines: soprano, tenor, and bass.

In traditional shape-note singing, the tenor (middle) line carries the melody and sopranos (top line) sing harmony or, in some hymns, sing the tenor line raised an octave. Basses (the bottom line) provide a second harmony. Later versions add a fourth line to be sung by altos, providing full four-part harmony (see fig. 6.3).

FIGURE 6.2. Original Three-Part Version of "Amazing Grace." Source: Sacred Harp Hymnal, Google Books.

FIGURE 6.3. A Later Four-Part Version of "Amazing Grace." Source: E.O. Excell, *Coronation Hymns* (1910).

In *Cooper v. James*, the court considered whether the addition of new alto lines to *Sacred Harp* hymns created original derivative works that could not be copied by a competitor.[16] Some of the more famous hymns harmonized by Cooper included "Bound for Canaan," "Jordan's Banks," "Nearer My God to Thee," "Rock of Ages," "Wayfaring Stranger," and "Wondrous Love," so the stakes were high when James published his competing edition. In rejecting Cooper's claim of copyright infringement, the court denied that the new alto lines were sufficiently original. The new harmonies were such that "a writer of music with experience and skill might readily make."[17]

The court in *Cooper* looked to an older case that employed a "mere mechanics" test to determine whether a new work was original. In other words, the alto lines were conventional, of the sort that any mechanic/technician of conventional harmony would compose. Given the rather rigid nature of the shape-note idiom (do some listening to *Sacred Harp* tunes on YouTube), an additional alto line would have been very strongly suggested by the preexisting tenor, soprano, and bass lines and therefore insufficiently original to its composer.

Cooper pairs nicely with another harmony case, *Tempo Music, Inc. v. Famous Music Corp.*[18] The case involved jazz greats Duke Ellington and Billy Strayhorn, who had collaborated on many tunes, including such standards as "Take the 'A' Train." After Strayhorn's death, a dispute arose between his estate and Ellington's estate over royalties earned by a famous composition, "Satin Doll." Ellington often played the song (with lyrics by Johnny Mercer) to end his band's shows. Strayhorn's primary contribution to the composition were its harmonies, but the court was unwilling to hold as a matter of law that harmony could never be original enough to merit a copyright. This was jazz, a traditionally unconventional genre. The court found that jazz "musicians frequently move beyond traditional rules to create a range of dissonant and innovative sounds."

The Ellington estate tried to argue that Strayhorn's harmonic contribution was merely the "formulaic application of centuries-old compositional rules," but the court rejected that position, finding that, in jazz, harmonies were not always the mere "mechanical by-product" of a melody. Put another way, a computer-savvy composer could write a program that would generate the predictable alto lines at issue in *Cooper*, but the same software program would never generate the unexpected and rule-bending Strayhorn harmonies.

Music cases in general are a great place to look for guidance in drawing the line between original (protected) and nonoriginal (unprotected) contributions. Music is also a category of work in which the public interest is strongly implicated. Music directors, especially in churches and community groups, often operate on tight budgets and, as a result, rely on the public domain as a source of royalty-free scores for their singers and instrumentalists. An erroneous claim of copyright by a music publisher has serious real-world consequences. Musicians are not only risk-averse and unlikely to ignore a false claim of copyright, but they often have a moral commitment to respecting copyright. After all, they are often composers and arrangers themselves. For that reason, they are especially likely to be intimidated by the false threat of litigation made by the fraudulent placement of a copyright symbol on the bottom of an unoriginal version of a public domain work.

Moreover, we cannot expect choir directors to toss aside a copyfraud score and find the original public domain version to use instead. Few directors have access to libraries well stocked with historical scores. I live in a town with a large public university that has a good music school, so I was able to track down an original version of "*O Bone Jesu*," but most musicians are not so lucky. Music directors need to be able to confidently ignore fraudulent copyright symbols and use their photocopy machines and scanners.

What we hear and where our money goes is directly influenced by copyfraud, so let's spend a bit more time on the law of originality as it pertains to music.

Piano Reductions

Very frequently, orchestral and choral compositions are reduced to versions that are written for a keyboard. Sometimes, the reduction is highly mechanical. For example, one could easily write the four vocal lines in *Amazing Grace* to look like a two-staved piano score, so that it would be slightly easier to play (most good pianists can just look at a four-staved choral score and play the vocal lines without a formal written reduction). Such a routine adjustment would be unoriginal and unprotectable. On the other hand, converting a complex symphonic work to a version playable on a piano may be a different story. In *Wood v. Boosey*, for example, the court considered a keyboard reduction of the opera *The Merry Wives of Windsor* and found the arrangement to be sufficiently original.[19] Figure 6.4 shows a page from the overture's piano reduction.

FIGURE 6.4. *The Merry Wives of Windsor.* Source: IMSLP, Petrucci Music Library.

Choosing precisely how to reduce this score to something more easily playable on the piano is more difficult than tinkering with a simple four-part choral work. And this page is not the most complex or the most fully instrumented part of the opera. Plus, it lacks the vocal parts. The English court in *Wood v. Boosey* found that writing a keyboard reduction of the *Merry Wives of Windsor* was not merely a mechanical enterprise.

Currently, US originality cases assess the number, quality, and nature of independent choices made by the creator of the derivative work. So, if the composer of the piano score to the *Merry Wives of Windsor* had to exercise significant independent judgment in producing a score for the keyboard, then the reduction would likely be protectable. But if 10 composers commissioned to perform the same reduction would all do it in more or less the same way, this would be evidence that the reductions were the result of convention rather than original choices. Interestingly, a UK court might be willing to find originality even in the absence of independent choices made by an "author." Unlike US law, UK law rewards the "sweat of the brow" (the artist's labor) with copyright, and in *Wood v. Boosey*, it might have been enough that the writer of the piano reduction expended significant labor on it. *Wood v. Boosey* presents a nice example, but it is not necessarily persuasive precedent in the US.

Rekeying, Recleffing, and Typeface

Arguments over the piano reduction of the *Merry Wives of Windsor* don't really implicate copyfraud. The author of the reduction probably believed that he had done something original. The troubling cases involve much more spurious claims to copyright. For example, arrangers will frequently change the key of a public domain work. Converting a piece written in A-flat major to E-flat major is entirely mechanical and can be done by any decent bit of music software. Same with changing a line written in G clef to C clef. Any publisher claiming copyright in these sorts of changes is lying, plain and simple.

In a similar vein, music publishers will frequently change the typeface of a public domain work to a more modern font. As helpful as such an adjustment might be to musicians, it is hardly the sort of original contribution worthy of copyright protection. Unfortunately, in some European countries, a change in typeface can confer legal rights to the new publisher. For this reason, the German edition of a public domain work may contain a copyright symbol, even if the new edition is otherwise identical to the original historical work. US musicians are slowly learning to ignore this use of the copyright symbol, which is not respected by US law.

Editorial Cleanup (Dynamic Markings, Meter, Ties, and Bar Lines)

Arrangers of public domain music often go beyond purely mechanical acts like those just described. Arrangers can add editorial markings not present on the original historical score, and they may even change the meter (rhythm). This is particularly true of music from the medieval, Renaissance, and early Baroque periods, when composers frequently wrote only notes, leaving the interpretation of the text to the instrumentalists. The extent to which changes to historical scores are protectable depends on the quality of the arranger's creative choices.

For example, Walter Murphy, an American composer famous for his work on *Buffy the Vampire Slayer*, *Family Guy*, and *American Dad*, produced a disco version of Beethoven's *Fifth Symphony* in 1976 that hit number one on the US charts. This sort of rhythmic contribution could well be protectable. Murphy changed the piece in unexpected and creative ways. He certainly was not intentionally lying to the public when he claimed a copyright in his arrangement. But what about a devious music publisher who makes much more minor changes in an attempt to justify the use of the copyright symbol?

The typical Gregorian chant contains no rhythmic or dynamic markings like *fff* ("get super loud") or *pp* ("get really soft"). For centuries, choral directors have made their own choices about when the music should speed up, slow down, get louder, or get softer. Given traditional expectations on how this ancient musical idiom should be performed, the space available for creative choices by an arranger are pretty narrow, although Walter Murphy might come up with some creative disco versions. Should an arranger who decides to mark up the medieval score with the occasional *andante, ritardando, poco accelerando, forte,* or *mezzo piano* be entitled to copyright?

The answer is certainly no. Such choices are not original in the legal sense. Protecting such an annotated score would lead to the absurd result that a choir director making the same choices (many of which are virtually dictated by centuries of performance practice) might infringe the new arranger's performance right. Copyright is a strict liability offense—meaning that you can accidently violate somebody's copyright. In the world as claimed by music publishers, a wholly innocent director who sped up or slowed down (or amplified or hushed) her choir in the same way as indicated by some remote, unknown, prior arranger might be a copyright infringer.

Nah. The law is not that stupid.

The same applies to other sorts of minor changes, like the addition of bar lines (the horizontal line that divides music into measures) or slurs (the tying of two notes together with a curved line). A lot of early music was written without bar lines; adding bar lines makes it easier for the modern musician to read but adds nothing truly original to a piece. Regardless of when a piece was originally composed, the modern addition of slur marks and other notations, such as fingering suggestions, are meant to tweak a performance in a particular direction or make it easier to play, not to make an original contribution to the composition.

By putting a copyright symbol on the bottom of a piece of public domain music, publishers are almost always implicitly claiming that changing a key or typeface or adding dynamic markings, rhythmic notations, slurs, or bar lines have magically converted a free work into a proprietary one. They are not only wrong; they are deliberately misleading the public.

One should note that a critical score, extensively annotated by the new arranger, could contain original contributions. Consider a new edition of Shakespeare's *Hamlet* that provides an introduction to the work and peppers every page with useful information about the meaning of Shakespeare's language, biographical information about the characters, and suggestions for staging. No one can copyright Shakespeare's prose, so anyone can extract the original language from the new edition, but the significant new material original to the editor will be protected. You should not photocopy such a book! Some massively annotated critical editions exist in the music world and may also be protected.

Music experts can help laypeople understand what is sufficiently original and worthy of protection. Close calls certainly exist, but in the typical case of a music publisher making minor editorial additions, even the layperson can smell the stench of copyfraud.

How to Sue the Bastards

The attentive reader will not be surprised that while tracking down images for this chapter, I found many claims to copyright in *Amazing Grace*, even though it fell into the public domain long ago.

Jason Mazzone and I do not use the word "fraud" lightly. In the civil context, a person commits fraud by intentionally or recklessly misleading a reasonable person to the benefit of the person perpetrating the falsehood. This is precisely what a publisher does when it intentionally claims copyright in a minor addition (or nonaddition) to a public domain work. It intends the public to rely on the misrepresentation, refrain from copying, and make a purchase (or pay a royalty) to its benefit. Since this behavior is illegal, I'll identify four ways for victims to bring suit against publishers.[20]

Breach of Warranty. The narrowest grounds for suing a publisher applies primarily to a licensee who discovers that it has purchased a license from someone falsely (or even negligently) claiming copyright. The paradigm case is *Tams-Witmark Music Library v. New Opera Co.*, involving *The Merry Widow* opera by Franz Lehar.[21] New Opera paid more than $50,000 to Tams-Witmark for a license to perform the opera in the US. The work, however, had already passed into the public domain at the time of the contract. In other words, New Opera could have performed the work for free. When it discovered this and stopped paying royalties, Tams-Witmark sued. In response, New Opera made a claim for its money back. The New York court essentially held that Tams-Witmark had breached its contract by incorrectly claiming to own the copyright. It was ordered to pay back any royalties it had received from New Opera.

The *Merry Widow* case suggests why Getty Images is careful not to claim copyright ownership in the public domain images it licenses. It collects licensing fees for the use of public domain images, but it does not state, "We own the copyright." In fact, charging for access to a high-resolution public domain image is certainly permissible (think of the Louvre selling you a postcard of the Mona Lisa). Getty provides one-stop shopping for customers and sometimes conserves images that are difficult or impossible to find. The situation may be different when Getty does more than just sell a download. By using the term "license" and setting terms for yearly use, Getty may imply that it has rights to the image. By charging a differential rate for various sorts of uses (for posters, brochures, uses on commercial websites, nonprofit uses), Getty implies that it is doing more than just selling a copy of an image.

Imagine the Louvre charging you $10,000 a year to use the Mona Lisa on your Leonardo da Vinci tribute website.

Regardless of what a person thinks about the Getty business model, a breach of warranty claim against Getty is harder to make than against Tams-Witmark, which used the copyright symbol and claimed ownership of the work. As with Tams-Witmark, any claim against Getty would have to be contractual. Getty would need to breach a promise (implied or express). In general, the breach of warranty cause of action is most useful in licensing cases, where the victim relies on the seller's representation of ownership. Other causes of action can be brought in situations where there is no contract or license.

Unjust Enrichment/Restitution. The law of unjust enrichment and restitution provides a broader ground for relief to victims of copyfraud. Neither remedy requires that the victim have entered into a contract with the perpetrator. The basic idea behind them resonates with most people's sense of justice: someone who remits money in reliance on a misrepresentation should be able to recover that money. Section 24 of the *Restatement of Restitution* states the principle clumsily in this way: "[A] right to restitution exists in favor of a person who, erroneously believing because of a mistake of fact that another has a right, title, or power . . . and induced by such mistake has paid money to the other."[22]

In the copyfraud context, consider a consumer (e.g., musician or teacher or employee) who needs multiple copies of a public domain text, which could be a book, poem, play, song, recipe, photograph, magazine article, or map. Ignorant of copyright law and wanting to be a good citizen, the potential copier is deterred by the copyright symbol, which is often accompanied by an express warning:

WARNING!!!

This computer is being used to illegally copy material in violation of federal law! Your computer records have been noted and can be used in court.

Or:

COPYING IS ILLEGAL AND PUNISHABLE BY FINES UP TO $100,000 PER VIOLATION!

Understandably, potential copiers will frequently purchase multiple copies rather than risk breaking the law. In circumstances involving the photocopying of books and magazine articles, the copier may choose to pay the Copyright Clearance Center an outrageous per page sum for the right to copy. For example, I just visited the Copyright Clearance Center website and requested permission to copy 20 pages from Alexander Hamilton's and John Jay's *Federalist Papers*, a key historical document long in the public domain. I pretended to be a law professor (wait, I am a law professor) needing to create an electronic course pack for 100 students in my constitutional law class. According to the Copyright Clearance Center, I should pay it $403.50 for the right to provide these free, public domain materials to my students.

And we wonder why the cost of getting a higher education is so high.

Okay, the legal principle is clear: people who reasonably rely on a misrepresentation and pay money are entitled to their money back. But if the law is unambiguous, why do publishers continue to make claims to public domain material?

Because they can. Because there is no adequate disincentive to make erroneous claims.

Lawyers are expensive, and mistaken payments made to places like the Copy-right Clearance Center are usually not large enough to warrant hiring legal help. Before my wife met me, she would sometimes buy 30 copies of a public domain work rather than ignore the copyright symbol and photocopy. At three dollars per copy, her total expenditures were less than $100—a good chunk of her church's sheet music budget, but not enough to engage an attorney and obtain a refund.

And remember, the remedy in a case of unjust enrichment is merely the return of the victim's payment.

What do the liars have to lose?

Civil Fraud. Fraud requires "the intent that a representation shall be made, that it shall be directed to a particular person or class of persons, that it shall convey a certain meaning, that it shall be believed, and that it shall be acted upon in a certain way."[23] This is precisely the case when a music publisher places a copyright symbol on a public domain work to which it has made only insignificant changes. The symbol is intended to convey a "certain meaning" ("We have rights to this—don't copy it!"), and the publisher definitely wants its statement to be believed and acted upon. The copyright symbol is "acted upon" when the consumer refrains from copying and buys a license or pays for multiple copies. Reckless disregard for the truth can also constitute fraud.

An action for fraud has more far-reaching consequences than breach of warranty or unjust enrichment because the victim might receive punitive damages. In Georgia, where I first uncovered the practice of falsely claiming copyright, punitive damages can be awarded for "willful misconduct, malice, *fraud*, wantonness, oppression or that entire want of care which would raise the presumption of conscious indifference to consequences."[24]

Bingo.

So, shouldn't the prospect of punitive damages scare publishers into amending their practices?

Not so much.

First, some publishers' attorneys may have (wrongly) advised their clients that a claim to copyright based on minor editorial changes is valid. In fact, one attorney for a major music publisher told me that such claims are standard practice. A publisher relying on advice of counsel can plausibly claim not to be intentionally lying. Second, most consumers aren't aware of the rip-off and don't know to complain. Third, fraud is a claim based on state law, while copy-right law is purely federal law. Few lawyers are experts in both subjects, and at-torneys apparently have not connected the dots. Fourth, punitive damages are usually awarded as a multiplier of the actual damage done to the victim. Even a 100x multiplier of a $50 mistaken payment is pretty small, just $5,000, maybe not even enough to pay an attorney.

Unfortunately, I cannot personally initiate a test case against music publish-ers because I know the law and therefore couldn't "reasonably rely" on a falsely applied copyright symbol.

False Advertising. State statutes banning false advertising may provide the greatest promise to victims of copyfraud. Almost all states prohibit "unfair meth-ods of competition and unfair acts or practices"[25] and incorporate by reference a variety of federal regulations forbidding false advertising. The basic rule of the Federal Trade Commission states that to qualify as deceptive::

1. a representation must be likely to mislead the consumer;
2. the representation must be viewed from the perspective of the reasonable consumer; and
3. the representation must be material.[26]

Note that these three conditions do not include bad intent; there is no need to prove that the copyright symbol was used deliberately to mislead. Totally innocent mistakes are actionable. Thus, under this three-part test, the erroneous placement of the copyright symbol on public domain materials would seem to easily qualify as false advertising. A potential copier who respects the symbol and refrains from copying a public domain work has been misled, and unless the consumer knows that the symbol is being used falsely, he is certainly behaving reasonably. After all, we generally want consumers to respect the symbol and not copy. Finally, the use of the copyright symbol is "material." Consumer reliance on the symbol must have an actual negative effect on the consumer. Of course, the primary reason to use the copyright symbol is to deter potential copiers and induce them to pay for a license or multiple copies. Little wonder that one of the rare relevant cases found that "invalid copyright registrations are *per se* violations" of false advertising law.[27]

Unfortunately, federal law does not provide a class-action mechanism that could be deployed against publishers that routinely commit copyfraud.

Consumers lack standing to enforce federal false advertising law, and federal diversity jurisdiction class actions based on state law require minimum damages of $50,000 per claimant, which would almost never be met in a copyfraud case. In the absence of a class action, false advertising law will not significantly deter copyfraud. Two prominent commentators explain:

> The major obstacle preventing purchasers from policing market deception through legal action is the difference in the relative gains between the purchaser and the seller in winning a lawsuit. In many instances, the costs of litigation to the consumer will far exceed the amount of the harm suffered from the deception and accordingly the amount of recovery in the event of success.[28]

In the absence of the ability to aggregate multiple claims against publishers, the economics of litigation clearly favor a publisher committing copyfraud.

Although underutilized, state law class-action provisions provide a glimmer of hope to the victims of false misrepresentations. Consumers have standing to bring suit, and minimum monetary injury requirements are generally not imposed on each potential class member. The Illinois Court of Appeals, for example, affirmed class-action status to victims of misrepresentations regarding advertised charges for muffler installations.[29] Another Illinois court allowed a class action to proceed against a fast-food chain that allegedly misrepresented the beefiness of its sandwiches.[30] Other suits incorporate the same logic.[31]

As of the publication of this book, no major class action has been brought against publishers who routinely commit copyfraud. Perhaps a chance meeting between a class-action lawyer and a copyright lawyer in a bar will spark a conversation and a revolution. Or maybe not. The copyright lawyer is more likely to represent publishers than choir directors.

CHAPTER SEVEN

A PICTURE IS WORTH A THOUSAND CLICK-THROUGHS

How the Absence of Copyright Adds Value

IN 2013, the UK government announced that any further changes to UK intellectual property law, including copyright, would have to be justified on the basis of objective, empirical evidence.[1] The goal is to let data, rather than lobbyists' wishes, drive UK policy. Interestingly, copyright owners in the UK have not squawked too loudly. They already collect a lot of data on their positive impact on the economy and can quantify this data for policymakers. In fact, estimates of the contribution of the creative industries to the UK economy range as high as £92 billion per year.[2]

No one doubts that creative contributions generate massive economic value, and no one doubts that copyright law incentivizes the production and commercialization of many works, but we should pause before concluding that copyright law drives *all* profits earned by the creative industries. A lot of creativity occurs in the absence of copyright and, as we shall see, *because* of its absence.

Take, for example, rock deities the Grateful Dead, who famously let fans record and share the group's music for free. The band generated a lot of goodwill and made piles of money charging audiences to listen to their live concerts.[3] Copyright law was basically irrelevant to the band. Even harder-headed creators rationally give away their works for free. The entire open-access software industry is built on "kernels" of freely copiable code, with firms like Red Hat earning significant profits from service and customization contracts instead of copyright. The Creative Commons[4] contains more than a billion works to copy and share, including over 58 million images distributed by Wikimedia Commons.[5]

Wikipedia is an example of an extremely valuable creation that is indifferent to copyright. In 2013, a very rough calculation estimated that the website was worth tens of billions of dollars.[6] Wikipedia, of course, places no reliance on copyright law. Its content is open for all to use and copy.

This doesn't mean that copyright law is doing no work in the economy. It's really important, but crediting *all* the profits earned by the creative industries to copyright law is hopelessly naïve.

Moreover, the *absence* of copyright may generate value, especially when the creative industries use public domain works as the basis for creation. For example, making a movie based on a copyrighted book requires permission (which may or may not be granted) and the payment of a licensing fee. As you will remember from chapter 4, when Disney makes *Snow White* or *Cinderella* or *Aladdin* or *The Little Mermaid* or *Pocahontas*, it has neither concern. What's the value of free access to Disney?

In light of industry estimates of the value of their copyrights, the UK Intellectual Property Office (IPO) recognized a need for an estimate of the value of the public domain, or at least some part of it, to creators and to consumers. For years, copyright professors have insisted that nurturing a vibrant public domain is critical to the creative industries, but hard numbers on the value of free access were lacking.

Prompted by the IPO's challenge, my friends at CREATe (the Centre for Copyright and New Business Models in the Creative Economy at the University of Glasgow) set out on the difficult task of quantifying the value of the *absence* of legal protection to creators. We decided to focus on public domain images. Along the way we discovered some shocking consumer rip-offs perpetrated by Corbis and Getty Images, and we reverse-engineered the Google search algorithm.

Public Domain Images on Wikipedia

We studied public domain images used on Wikipedia pages, largely because the website is so transparent about the source and timing of its contributions.

For example, if you go to author Stephen King's page on Wikipedia and right-click on his photo, you get full information about the legal status of the image. You will learn that the photographer, "pinguino," dedicated it to the public for copying, sharing, and remixing under a Creative Commons 2.0 license that requires any user to properly attribute "pinguino" as the source. The title of the jpeg file suggests that the picture was taken at the 2007 New York Comic-Con.

Our first task was to determine the extent to which public domain images were being used on Wikipedia, and we started with 365 authors who at one time had a novel on the end-of-year, top 10 *New York Times* bestsellers list. We identified the Wiki page for each writer, along with the source and provenance of each photo (when there was one). We also gathered biographical information and data on the number of times each page had been visited.

Our first finding was quite counterintuitive: the older the author (in terms of when he or she was born), the *more* likely that his or her Wiki page contained an image (see fig. 7.1).

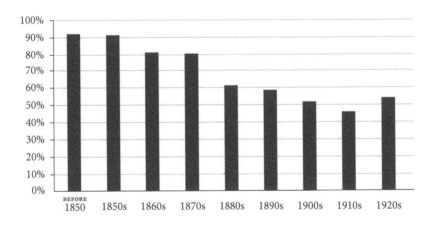

■ Percentage with Image on Wiki Page

FIGURE 7.1. Bestselling Authors by Date of Birth. Source: Updated from Paul J. Heald, Kristopher Erickson, and Martin Kretschmer, "The Valuation of Public Domain Works: A Case Study of Public Domain Images on Wikipedia," *Harvard Journal of Law and Technology* 29 (2015): 16.

Given that photography was more common in the twentieth century than in the nineteenth, why did only about 50 percent of the youngest set of best-selling authors, some of whom are alive today, have images on their Wiki pages, while more than 90 percent of forgotten authors born before 1860 have images on their pages?

At the time I wrote this book, you could encounter Harold Frederic (1856–98), whose book *The Damnation of Theron Ware* was a bestseller in 1896, two years after his untimely and sensational death. After he suffered a stroke, his mistress, Kate Lyon, an avid Christian Scientist, allegedly convinced him to ignore his doctor. Frederic should have stopped smoking cigars, swilling beer and liquor, and eating red meat after the stroke; however, his stubborn refusal may have been due to his hatred of physicians, rather than a newfound allegiance to Lyon's Christian Scientism. After he died, Lyon, with whom Frederic had two children, was charged with manslaughter, but she was acquitted in a headline-making trial. Brigit Bennet's biography of Frederic is entitled somewhat luridly, but perhaps appropriately, *The Damnation of Harold Frederic.*[7] Despite his interesting life, Frederic is now a rather obscure character, known mainly to historians of late nineteenth-century literature. Despite his obscurity, his Wiki page is graced with the image of a distinguished gentleman sporting an outstanding walrus moustache.

Contrast Frederic's page with that of Mary Stewart (1916–2014), who was born Mary Florence Elinor Rainbow (her father was a vicar, the Reverend Fred Rainbow). Her retelling of the Arthurian legend in *The Crystal Cave* (1970), *The Hollow Hills* (1973), and *The Last Enchantment* (1979) continues to charm millions of readers. An early bestselling novel, *The Moonspinners* (1962), was made into a successful Disney movie in 1964, starring Haley Mills and Eli Wallach. Photographs of her can be found on the Internet, including one from a Google image search that reveals a grandmotherly woman in front of a beautiful loch (along with some intriguing photos of her younger self). But (as I write this book) no Wiki page builder had dared to add an image for her fans.

Copyright law provides the easiest explanation of this situation. Frederic died in 1898, so any image of him published during his lifetime is in the public domain. Stewart didn't publish a novel until 1954, so any photos of her are much more likely to be under copyright. Wiki page builders are therefore stymied.

In general, the persistence of copyright in post-1923 photographs probably explains why older nineteenth-century bestselling authors like Maurice Stockton, Paul Ford, Ian Maclaren, and Vaughn Kester (and many others you've never heard of) almost all have Wiki page images, while newer and even better-selling authors do not. As of 2018, some recognizable names in the image-missing category included James Gould Cozzens (*By Love Possessed*), Richard Llewellen (*How Green Was My Valley*), Irving Stone (*Lust for Life*; *The Agony and the Ecstasy*), Irving Wallace (*The Fan Club*), and Morris West (*Shoes of the Fisherman*).

A similar lack of images plagues the Wiki page of Sloan Wilson (1920–2003), who wrote several bestselling books that were made into successful movies, such as *The Man in the Gray Flannel Suit* in 1956 (starring Gregory Peck, Jennifer Jones, and Frederic March) and *A Summer Place* in 1959 (whose theme song spent nine weeks at number one on the Billboard singles chart in 1960). Wilson is also interesting for a more obscure reason. Ted Kaczynski, the infamous Unabomber, severely injured Percy Wood, the head of United Airlines, by hiding a bomb inside Wilson's novel *The Icebrothers* and sending it to Wood's home in Lake Forest, Illinois, in 1980.[8]

Even while the copyright status of photos of Sloan Wilson or Mary Stewart frustrates Wiki page builders, a huge reservoir of public domain photos exists for other authors: those who were photographed before 1923 and those whose images are in the public domain for reasons other than term expiration. Joseph Conrad (1857–1924), the author of *Lord Jim* and *The Heart of Darkness*, is pictured on his Wiki page with a photo from 1904 whose copyright has long expired. The Wiki page of Philip Roth (1933–2018), winner of the National Book Award for Fiction and author of *Goodbye, Columbus*, among numerous other bestsellers, has a nice photo of taken in 1973. Luckily for Roth fans, the photo was published without the required copyright notice and is therefore in the public domain (as is the photo on Jacqueline Susan's Wiki page).

The photos on the Wiki pages of Ernest Hemingway, William Faulkner, and John Steinbeck are in the public domain because the original copyright owner failed to make the required renewal filing for photos taken before 1964. Without a renewal certificate, any work dating from 1964 or before entered the public domain 28 years after its publication.

The pencil sketch of Leon Uris (*Exodus; Trinity*) found on his Wiki page is in the public domain for a different reason: its creator donated it to the public domain through a Creative Commons license. Some photographers are happy to eschew copyright and voluntarily increase the supply of images available for free public use. The Wiki pages of Gore Vidal, Saul Bellow, Michael Crichton, Herman Wouk, and Daphne du Maurier all have photos dedicated to the public domain by the photographer.

Figure 7.2 shows the breakdown of legal justifications offered by Wiki page builders for images of 371 bestselling authors born between 1895 and 1965. The three justifications shown right-most in the chart together accounted for almost 80 percent of author images used. Although Wikipedia frowns on fair use justifications, 13 percent of page builders rely on it anyway. A final 7 percent of images were used with permission of the copyright owner, without a complete dedication of the work to the public domain. For example, Carl Van Vechten, a famous photographer and novelist (his 1926 bestseller *Nigger Heaven* was praised by some members of the Harlem Renaissance and reviled by others), donated 1,395 photographs to the Library of Congress in 1966 with restrictions on their use expiring in 1986.[9] A number his photos, including those of Franz Werfel (*Song of Bernadette*) and Gertrude Stein ("There is no there, there") appeared among the author pages in the sample.

Clearly, many Wiki pages have images only because of the absence of copyright protection. Just as obviously, an image adds value to a page. A reader wants to see the subject of a biographical page. On insect, animal, or plant pages, an

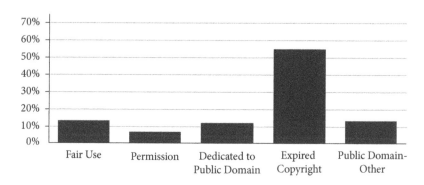

FIGURE 7.2. Justifications for Image Use on Wikipedia. Source: Heald, Erickson, and Kretschmer, "Valuation of Public Domain Works," 18.

image is even more important. Same with pages describing places and events. Imagine trying to communicate the bombing of Hiroshima or Nagasaki without a photo of the devastation.

A picture may be worth a thousand words, but how should one quantify the value of an image that graces a Wiki page due to the lack of copyright?

We considered two possible ways to measure the value of public domain photos on Wikipedia. First, we recognized that the availability of a free image saves money. No licensing fee need be paid, and the expense of negotiating is also saved. So, one could equate the value of a public domain photo by measuring how much more it would cost to use a copyrighted image.

A more direct measure of the value that a photo adds to a Wiki page might be measured in terms of the extra visits to the page attracted by the addition of the image. Conventional wisdom holds that the Google search algorithm prioritizes pages with images over pages without images. Webpage builders are frequently advised "to increase traffic to your page by adding an image."[10] For this reason, we measured the increase in traffic to Wiki pages after an image was added and estimated the potential advertising value generated by the additional page views.

But first ...

Cost Savings and How Getty Images Sells the Brooklyn Bridge

Calculating the costs saved by using a free image over a copyrighted image is fairly easy. In 2014, we found the image of British author Rudyard Kipling shown in figure 7.3. This public domain photo is free from Wikimedia Commons. At the time our research was initially conducted, Corbis was charging $105/year and Getty Images $117/year for a web license for the image. When Getty absorbed Corbis, the license price went up to £39 for three months, about $220/year (see fig. 7.4).

The author of *The Jungle Book* might have been amused that the largest purveyors of photographs in the world would license a free public domain picture of him for more than $200/year. Kipling certainly had a sense of humor. He famously wrote to a magazine that had erroneously reported his death, "I've just read that I am dead. Don't forget to delete me from your list of subscribers."[11] We don't know what he would have thought about the caption on what *The Guinness Book of Records* once claimed was the bestselling postcard of all time:

FIGURE 7.3. Public Domain Photo of Rudyard Kipling. Source: Wikimedia Commons.

"Do you like Kipling?"

"I don't know, you naughty boy, I've never kippled!"

Purchasers of a Getty license to use the Kipling photo, however, will not be amused to learn they could have downloaded it for free from Wikimedia Commons.[12] The photo is an orphan, so it's difficult to tell exactly why it's in the public domain. It appears to have been taken before 1925, the current date before which no published work is protected in the US. If it was taken between 1925 and Kipling's death in 1936, I can find no relevant renewal record.[13]

The least-amused group are photographers who dedicate their photos to the public domain only to see Getty Images license the same photos to the public for a fee. Carol Highsmith, a photographer who donated almost 20,000 photos to the Library of Congress, was incensed to learn that Getty was licensing her photos. Even worse, she was sent a letter by Getty stating that she needed to buy a license to use her own photographs![14] She responded with a $1 billion lawsuit against the photo-licensing giant, which did not stop its practice of licensing public domain photographs. Her copyright claims against Getty were dismissed because she no longer owned the copyrights and had no standing. Her state law deceptive business practices claims were more plausible, but Getty settled those claims, which prevented them from being litigated.[15]

Getty argued in the Highsmith case that commercializing public domain works was routine and that it was behaving no differently than a publisher who produces and sells a new edition of a public domain book like *David Copperfield*. The problem is that Getty, unlike a book publisher, is selling not a tangible good but a license to use a work for a set period of time. Imagine Random House licensing the right to use the character of David Copperfield or granting permission to a film maker to produce a new version of a film based on the book. Rather than being a "routine business practice," claiming licensing rights for public domain works is more akin to selling permission to cross the Brooklyn Bridge.

Back to Calculating Cost Savings

Of the 371 author pages we studied, 25 contained public domain photos that were being licensed by Getty or Corbis, even though the same images were available for free at Wikimedia Commons. A further 104 author pages

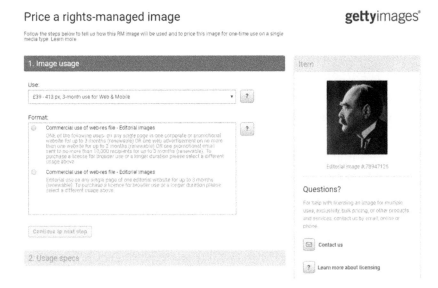

FIGURE 7.4. Screenshot of Getty Images Website. Source: Author (unpublished).

contained public domain photos that were similar to those licensed by Getty. In 2014, we calculated that the free availability of those 129 photos saved $77,400 in license fees over a five-year period (129 images ? $120 Getty yearly fee ? 5 years = $77,400). If Getty, after merging with Corbis in 2016, was charging $220/year for these photos (as per our Kipling example), then the five-year public domain cost savings rises to $141,900 for those 129 webpages.

The next challenge was to extrapolate these savings to Wikipedia as a whole. To do this, we hit the "random page" button on the Wikipedia home page 300 times. Fifty percent of the pages contained an image, and 87 percent of those images were from the public domain. At the time we did this, Wikipedia had about 4.6 million pages, meaning that an estimated 2 million pages contained public domain images (assuming the random page button really gives a random page). If each image was protected by copyright and needed a $220/year Getty-style license, then the use of free public domain images saved around $440 million per year.

As dramatic as that figure seems, we are fairly certain that it overestimates the costs saved. Why? Were Wikipedia to pay for images (it doesn't), it would have serious bargaining power with licensors. It is not a tiny web design firm that cannot negotiate a better price from folks like Getty. We suspect that Wikipedia could convince licensors to lower their rates. So, it's difficult to know precisely what the real savings might be.

Either way, it's not chump change.

Finally, Erickson, Perez, and Perez expanded on our research by tracking the use of 10,000 images randomly chosen from the 45 million public domain files available on Wikimedia Commons.[16] They detected more than 54,000 downstream uses of the images. Using a cost-savings approach similar to the one used above, they calculated a total value for all the millions of Wikimedia images at approximately $28.9 billion.

Definitely not chump change.

Advertising Value of Increased Traffic Flow

Estimating the value of traffic driven to Wiki pages by public domain images was harder (but more fun!) because we had to reverse-engineer the Google search algorithm that drives 95 percent of traffic on the web.[17] Unfortunately, we couldn't just compare the amount of traffic going to pages that have images and those that don't. At the time I'm writing this, I see that the Wiki page of Ernest Hemingway, which contains a public domain image, has received 180,599 views in the last three weeks. Over the same period, only 582 people have viewed the imageless webpage of Will James, a Newberry Medal winner for *Smokey the Cowhorse* (1927) (and who served 15 months in prison for cattle rustling).

It would be foolish to conclude that the difference in page views is due to the lack of an image on James's page rather than the mammoth popularity of Hemingway's books. To estimate the attractive power of images on a Wiki page, as opposed to the attractiveness of the subject matter of the Wiki page, one has to compare apples to apples. Therefore, we paired authors who were of similar popularity to determine whether the presence of an image increased the flow of traffic to a page. For example, we paired Will James (542 page views March–May 2009) with Gwen Davis (544 page views over the same three months).

Since we've already heard some of James's backstory, let's note that Gwen Davis was the defendant in one of the most sensational lawsuits in American literary history. Her book *Touching* (1971) told the sordid tale of a Santa Claus–like therapist with a PhD in psychology who . . . well . . . here's what the book's blurb on Amazon says:

> They have come to the Nude Encounter Group, desperately seeking escape from their own sexual hells: Soralee—the super-girl with too much of everything . . . Marion—a liberated woman in the office, but not in the bedroom . . . Nick—a frightened child hiding in a stud's body . . . The Minister—is his congregation ready for his radical concept of love? And above them all towers the enigmatic figure of Dr. Simon Herford—half charlatan, half genius, he calls the signals in a 20-hour sensuality marathon where the stakes are total sexual freedom—or destruction.[18]

Davis was sued by E. Paul Bindrim, a California therapist, who treated his patients in warm pools during "nude marathons."[19] Although Bindrim was hairless and lacked a PhD at the time the book was written, he managed to acquire a head of jolly white hair, a beard, and a mail-order PhD by the time of the trial. The physical transformation was enough to win his defamation suit against Davis and prompted Davis's publisher to sue her in turn.

In any event, neither James nor Davis had a picture on their Wiki pages in 2009, but Davis gained an image in 2011. Similarly, we paired other authors who appeared to be equally popular before one of their pages gained an image. Then we counted the page views of each author during the periods before and after one of them gained an image. We also matched pairs of composers and lyricists from another large database to increase the number of comparisons. When the dust settled, we estimated that the addition of an image was responsible for a roughly 19 percent increase in traffic to a page.

Are we absolutely certain of the 19 percent figure? Some of the data is quite "noisy," meaning factors other than the presence of an image could influence the number of visitors to a page. In a large sample, those blips should be fairly evenly spread among all authors, but the volatility of some of our observations reduce our confidence. But even if the actual influence of an image on traffic is a 5–10 percent increase, the collective value added by the images is impressive, as demonstrated below.

Here's how we eventually quantified the traffic value of *all* public domain images on Wikipedia: first, remember that in 2015, 2 million Wiki pages contained public domain images. And remember the 300 random pages we generated? The pages averaged about 18,966 views per year. If that's a good estimate of yearly views for the average Wiki page, then the 2 million pages with public domain images were visited more than 37 billion times that year.

That's a lot of page views, but recent statistics show even higher numbers in more recent years.[20]

But what is a Wikipedia page view worth? Wikipedia doesn't sell advertising space, so we have no actual market price, but other comparable services on the web do charge advertisers a fee for each page view, so it's not too hard to estimate what Wikipedia would be able to charge. A number of firms have tried to value a Wiki page view to potential advertisers on Wikipedia, and the valuations range from a half cent to one cent per view.[21] We chose one of the lowest estimates,, which valued a Wiki page view at $.005.[22]

If Wikipedia could charge $.005 per page view, then the advertising value of those 37 billion views would be almost $200 million per year. But what percentage of that total revenue would be driven by the presence of a public domain image? If our earlier estimate of 19 percent is accurate, then we could credit 19 percent of the $200 million figure, or about $36 million per year, to the presence of public domain images. That bears repeating, the *absence* of copyright adding $36 million in value.

All of our numbers are a little fuzzy, but we can clearly see how the public domain increases the use of images on Wikipedia pages and how those extra images create significant value.

CHAPTER EIGHT

FOUR STARS AND ROTTEN TOMATOES

When Piracy Hurts and When It Doesn't

ALTHOUGH THIS BOOK IS SKEPTICAL of some copyright rules, it does not endorse piracy. Sure, the term of copyright is too long, and publishers who commit copyfraud should be publicly spanked, but that's not a reason to disregard valid copyrights in songs or movies and download them for free. I don't pirate works—and neither should you—but that doesn't mean we should blindly accept claims that online piracy has destroyed the creative industries. We should not evaluate proposed anti-piracy legislation unless we first examine the data relevant to the claim that the law should be radically changed to address the problem.

We must first acknowledge that piracy, primarily on the Internet, has sharply decreased music sales revenue. Figure 8.1 shows a strong correlation between the emergence in 2000 of Napster, one of the first widely embraced, illegal, peer-to-peer file-sharing programs, and revenues earned by sales of recorded music in millions of dollars (e.g., \$25,000 = \$2,500,000,000). The figure does not count artist revenue in every market, such as Internet radio royalties, synchronization licenses, merchandise sales, or concert earnings, but it does confirm the standard intuition that people who can get music for free will be less willing to pay for it.

If you doubt that peer-to-peer file sharing is the culprit, consider figure 8.2. At this point, some readers may conclude that something must be done! Illegal file sharing on the Internet is destroying the music business and must be stopped.

Is the Sky Really Falling?

Hold one thought for later. Figure 8.1 measures the decline in *gross* revenue from music sales. It does not measure *net* revenue (profits). This distinction is important because if costs to music producers have also dropped substantially, then profits to artists may not necessarily have been reduced. Before considering this possibility and other relevant changes in the music market, let's first look at piracy from the perspective of a cold-blooded economist. (Is there any other kind?)

Economists are not immediately outraged by data on industry revenue decline because such numbers represent only one side of the public welfare equation. Revenue statistics tell us how much copyright protection is worth to publishers and artists, but they fail to convey the value the public gains from consuming the pirated works. Teenagers downloading music without permission are behaving illegally, but they are enjoying their tunes. Their welfare has undeniably increased, and we can even place a monetary value on their consumption.[1]

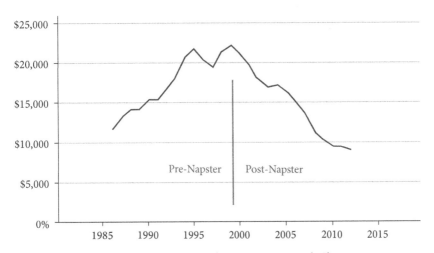

FIGURE 8.1. Decline in Music Revenue from Peer-to-Peer File Sharing, 1980–2015. Source: Joel Waldfogel, *Digital Renaissance: What Data and Economics Tell Us about the Future of Popular Culture* (Princeton, NJ: Princeton University Press, 2018).

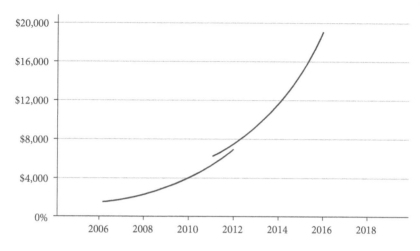

FIGURE 8.2. Increase in Peer-to-Peer File Sharing in Peta Bytes, 2004–2018. Source: Waldfogel, *Digital Renaissance.*

If consuming free music adds to welfare, then why do we forbid our kids to illegally download? For one thing, we may think that it's immoral (we'll revisit morality at the end of this chapter), and we don't want scofflaw children. Most important, we may worry that illegal downloading could so depress artist revenue that we will get fewer and lower-quality works in the future. That would be a true loss in public welfare.

Economists are dialed into this third concern—the potentially negative effect of piracy on creativity. They assume the purpose of copyright in the US is utilitarian, to maximize net public welfare and to incentivize the optimal amount of new creation for the optimal price. They want the law to calibrate copyright precisely, which might allow room for some unauthorized copying.

Here's an example. Twelve-year-old Pat's $10 per week allowance is spent entirely on music: 10 new downloads from iTunes every seven days. All of little Pat's income goes to music, and no amount of begging will pry any more cash loose from mom and dad. But Pat is a sneaky little snot and illegally downloads an extra 100 songs from the Internet every week without paying. How much damage has Pat caused to the music industry? How much income did artists lose? Zero. Pat could not have purchased the 100 additional songs because he lacked the money. No revenue was lost by artists at all.

In fact, little Pat might argue that his "piracy" is affirmatively efficient. It allows him to better identify the songs he has the ability to pay for, at no cost to the music industry.

In theory, economists would favor calibrating copyright law to accommodate all of Pat's downloading because it increases Pat's welfare at the expense of no one else. Industry estimates of its "lost revenue" are misleading because they count each illegal download as a lost full-priced sale, but that calculation is incorrect, as we see from Pat's story.

Economists are concerned about net public welfare. They envision a magic copyright balance wherein artists are adequately compensated and incentivized to create new works and consumers get sufficient access to reasonably priced artistic creations.

Fair enough, but how do we know the optimal amount of new music to be produced? How can we know whether consumers are paying too much? Or when their demand is satisfied? How do we know when music copyright raises prices and reduces output to the detriment of the public?

Currently, we have no idea whether music revenues are too high or too low to incentivize the "right" amount of music. Theoretical economists can show you some nifty algorithms, but problems in the real world (like the inability to perfectly figure out which consumers are willing to pay what price for which goods) entirely defeat their application to real music markets.

In the absence of data about how piracy affects artist incentives, the natural response to the lost revenue graph is to endorse some sort of reform. At a minimum, can't we be sure that less revenue means fewer new songs? And fewer new songs must be the wrong direction to go, even if we don't know the optimal number of new songs we should have. Reform is frequently advocated, either in the form of better enforcement or new substantive laws.

Less Theory and More Data

Helpfully, economists suggest we take a closer look at the music market before we endorse radical attempts to exterminate piracy. In particular, Professors Joel Waldfogel and Glynn Lunney, both ardent music lovers, have studied song production in the disruptive new world of illegal peer-to-peer file sharing. Here's what they found.

Waldfogel, currently the Frederick R. Kappel Chair in Applied Economics at the University of Minnesota, has studied the effect of illegal file sharing on the amount and quality of music production. Like others, he documents the connection between declining revenues from music sales and the increase in illegal music file sharing. Then, he asks whether the decline in revenue has led to a decline in the amount of music being produced. Has massive piracy resulted in diminished music production, something that would indicate the public welfare goals of music copyright are threatened?

His answer, surprisingly, is no. Although major labels have been releasing somewhat less music, Waldfogel finds "substantial growth in independent releases and self-released works of music relative to major label releases."[2] He notes that "[d]espite an absolute decline in major-label releases, the overall number of new works brought annually to market has increased by 50 percent since 2000." Lunney also examines the market and finds "the rise of file sharing and the parallel decline in record sales has led to an increase, rather than a decrease, in the creation of new music."

Before we start scrambling for a theory to explain why the amount of music would increase during a period of massive piracy and revenue decline, we should consider whether the quality of the new music is any good. Artists, deprived of income from music sales, may be churning out garbage in the hope of scraping together a living threatened by pirates. An increase in the *amount* of music does not necessarily prove that public welfare has increased.

Waldfogel tackles the quality question head on. He identifies 88 different sources of rankings of music quality—"best of" lists created by *Rolling Stone*, *Pitchfork*, *SPIN*, Metacritic, Zagat, and many others—and builds a massive database of songs released before and after the peer-to-peer file-sharing revolution. By using airplay and sales statistics, he captures a large percentage of the music that Americans listened to from 1980 to 2010 and studies whether the post-Napster years (2000–2010) delivered us a steaming pile of audio doo-doo.

After rigorous statistical analysis of data on music quality from critics and data on music consumption from industry associations, Waldfogel finds no evidence that the quality of music produced since 2000 has declined. He concludes that "the annual number of new albums passing various quality thresholds has remained roughly constant since Napster." During a period of intense piracy "consumers have experienced no reduction in the volume of high-quality recorded music products and may indeed have experienced an increase in the service flow from new work." Understandably, Waldfogel calls this state of affairs "puzzling."

We might be tempted to conclude that musicians will produce music regardless of the financial incentives. After all, don't they need an outlet for all that angst? Waldfogel did not control for angst levels! Just kidding. Surely, musicians are just as sensitive to income decline as other professionals. So, we are still left with a puzzle.

New Theories and More Data

Consider three possibilities offered by Waldfogel to explain the conundrum:

1. Although gross industry revenues dropped, net profits remained stable, so artists made more or less the same amount of money before and after Napster.
2. Net profits fell, but new entrants with different business models operated more efficiently in delivering quality products.
3. Net profits fell, but artists substituted labor for leisure and became more productive to offset lost income.

Empirical research suggests that all three possibilities are not only plausible but interlocked.

The first two hypotheses require an understanding of why high-quality music continued to be produced after 2000. It turns out that the same wave of technological changes that made piracy so cheap and easy in the post-Napster era also lowered the cost of production, promotion, and distribution of original music. Technology facilitated entry into the market by independent labels with a new set of business models. Figures 8.3 to 8.6 illustrate significant changes in the music market that occurred as peer-to-peer file sharing ramped up. Piracy did not cause the rise of independent music labels, but both phenomena have their roots in parallel technological innovation.

The number of "indie" releases clearly increases after 2000, as figure 8.3 shows. And those independent releases are high quality, at least judging by their growing share of Billboard chart rankings (fig. 8.4). Indie labels also grabbed

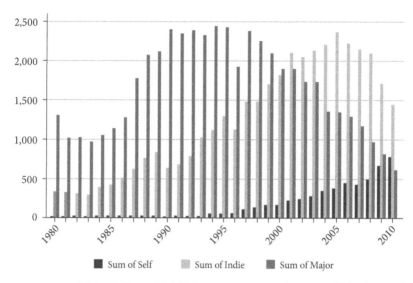

FIGURE 8.3. Major, Indie, and Self Releases, 1980–2010. Source: Waldfogel, *Digital Renaissance.*

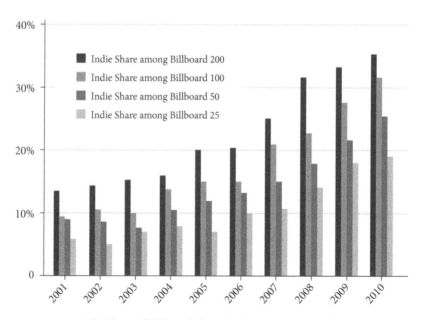

FIGURE 8.4. Indie Share of Billboard Chart Rankings, 2001–2010. Source: Waldfogel, *Digital Renaissance.*

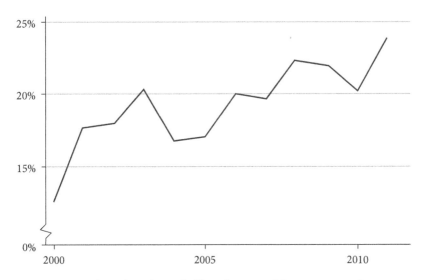

FIGURE 8.5. Independent Share of Billboard Top 200 Sales, 2000–2010. Source: Waldfogel, *Digital Renaissance*.

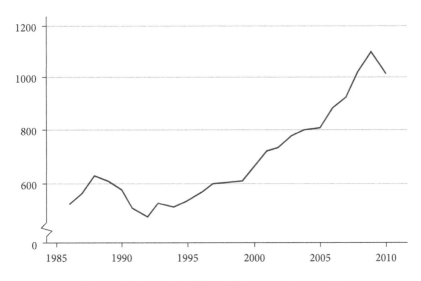

FIGURE 8.6. Distinct Artists on the Billboard Top 200, 1985–2010. Source: Waldfogel, *Digital Renaissance*.

an increasing share of the Billboard Top 200 sales (fig. 8.5). Not surprisingly, the success of independent producers also meant that more new and different artists hit the charts (fig. 8.6). It's not just the same singers from the same old labels any more. So, at the same time piracy was exploding, significant changes hit the music industry, a great productive shakeup of the old order, a true paradigm shift.

What Changed?

Once upon a time, large recording labels dominated the music industry. They worked hard to identify talented artists and then recorded their music. The most promising artists were promoted to the public, including the making of payments to radio stations to promote sales of recordings.[3] It was a top-down system with little or no scientific measuring of what the public actually wanted. The best a studio could do was learn from the past, attend to what succeeded and failed, and make informed guesses about what the public wanted next. According to Waldfogel, as many as 80 percent of albums made by the top labels failed to turn a profit.[4]

One reason so many albums failed was that the costs of talent identification, album creation, advertising/promotion, and distribution were high. Nowadays, a major talent, say, Justin Bieber, can be discovered just by surfing through YouTube (yes, you can blame YouTube).[5] Physically slogging from venue to venue in the old days was costly. Now, the digitization of music, collective buzz on social media, and appearance of multiple online platforms for talent have greatly increased the quality of information available to music production companies and thereby decreased talent discovery costs.

It's also cheaper now to record a song. Gone are the days when the only way to get a decent recording was to book time at a limited number of expensive professional recording studios. A good phone can record well enough to post a song on YouTube. Large industry players still use professional technicians and facilities, but since 2000, new hardware and software have greatly lowered the cost of making a composition into a saleable song. Costs have dropped both for major players like Sony and for independents like Dave Barbe's Chase Park Transduction Studio, one of four independent recording studios in my hometown of Athens, Georgia.

Just as important, advertising and promotion costs to music labels, large and small alike, have dropped since 2000. Before the era of YouTube, MySpace (remember them?), Facebook, Twitter, Instagram, and a host of other social media platforms, the most effective mode of promoting a musician was to convince radio stations and television variety shows to play his or her music, a process often requiring under-the-table payments to programmers. A fan base could also be created through extensive (and expensive) touring around the country. Without a doubt, radio airplay and touring remain key tools for promoting music, but as the graphics above suggest, independent labels with limited funds have successfully harnessed the Internet to build an audience without spending a lot of money. Not surprisingly, big labels are now using the same suite of low-cost social media tools.

Finally, distribution costs have dropped radically since 2000. In the last century, vinyl albums were pressed and compact discs encoded. Physical copies were shipped around the country. iTunes debuted in 2002, allowing consumers to purchase digital music directly for download. Other Internet services like Pandora and Spotify provide music to fee-paying listeners who control the playlist on their virtual jukebox. Simply put, getting notes from one place to another became a lot cheaper after 2000.

In other words, it's not entirely clear that *net* profits earned by artists from the exploitation of recorded music plummeted after 2000.

But What about the Counterfactual?

Waldfogel is convinced that rampant piracy has not harmed the music industry, but he admits that he cannot prove what would have happened after 2000 without file-sharing piracy ("the counterfactual"). Despite tons of unauthorized copying, the amount of music definitely went up, the quality was just as good, and more successful new artists appeared, but maybe we would have gotten even more music of even higher quality if all that piracy had not occurred. Would we have experienced a mega–golden age of song if pirates hadn't reduced overall revenue?

Maybe not. As we'll see below, at least one study suggests more money to artists doesn't necessarily mean more music.

Substituting Leisure for Labor

A recent book by Glynn Lunney (Texas A & M University) provides empirical evidence that an increase in artist revenue does not necessarily lead to more music.[6] In fact, he concludes the opposite is sometimes true.

His key insight is very simple and one well understood by economists and regular folks alike: once a worker acquires a certain level of wealth (and it varies for each person), she begins to substitute leisure for labor. Let's run a quick experiment. Give me $10 million, and let's see how long I stay in my current job. I mean it! Let's see what happens!

Lunney starts with an anecdote and then analyzes an impressive dataset. He illustrates the leisure-for-labor substitution point in the music context by reference to country music star Garth Brooks. With seven diamond-selling albums (one more than the Beatles), Brooks was the most successful country singer of the late 1980s and 1990s. Over $100 million in album sales made him fabulously wealthy, and he retired at the peak of his career in 2001, vowing not to record any new material until 2014. He didn't have to work, so he didn't.

If songwriters and singers are like normal people, then we should expect their output to decrease when they achieve a certain income level. My grandparents retired as soon as they could afford to—why should artists be any different?

I know what you're thinking. Artists *are* different. They are driven by the need to create or to quell their inner demons. But if we accept that argument, then we've weakened the rationale for music copyright itself, which rests on the premise that legal rights generating income are necessary for a healthy creative industry.

Lunney avoids the artists-are-different issue by studying a huge chunk of the music industry—not just Garth Brooks—to see how musicians behave in real life. He collected information about every top 50 song for each month from 1985 through 2013, giving him a multiyear snapshot of the periods before and after the file-sharing explosion in 1999–2000. He tracked when artists emerged, when they had hits (and how many), and whether they wrote their own music.

He accepted the conventional wisdom that artist revenue decreased substantially after 2000. So, according to his leisure/labor hypothesis, artist productivity should have risen due to the decrease in revenue. Musicians would have had to work harder and be more productive to make up for the lost income. This is the corollary of the labor/leisure substitution hypothesis. When they were making more money pre-2000, artists would have substituted leisure for labor and produced less. When harder times hit post-2000, they would have substituted labor for leisure.

After examining artists' productivity before and after 2000, Lunney concluded that musicians, like other workers, seem to be sensitive to the level of their income. Musicians reacted to rampant piracy by creating more music to make up for lost income. He estimated that piracy stimulated an increase of 48.4 more songs per year that spent at least one week in the top 50. Using a different statistical yardstick, he estimated that as many as 60.6 new top 50 songs per year may have been produced.

In other words, if the old regime had held, we may not, after all, have experienced a mega–golden age of music. According to Lunney, the precise opposite result is more likely. In the absence of piracy, musicians may have opted to substitute leisure for labor and produced less new music.

When Piracy Really Hurts

Despite the discussion above, we should not take a Pollyanna approach to piracy. Surely, declining revenues can have a negative effect on creativity. A starved-to-death artist isn't going to produce anything. Theoretically, piracy could have a crippling effect on a creative industry where the cost of producing a work is extremely high and the cost of copying is very low. If an artist cannot recover the cost of creation, he should be less likely to create. To test this theory, Rahul Telang and Joel Waldfogel studied the Indian (Bollywood) movie industry before and during a period of intense piracy that occurred from 1985 to 2000, during which time movie revenue in India fell by one-third to one-half. Unlike Waldfogel's music study, his work with Telang on Bollywood piracy shows the significantly negative effect of piracy on movie production.

A movie is the most expensive type of artwork to create, not infrequently costing more than $100 million to produce.[7] The investment risks are substantial, so the decision to make a movie is likely to highly depend on its income-earning potential. If massive piracy reduces the expected return on investment, we should see diminished production incentives. During the darkest days of movie piracy in India, the diminished prospects for profit negatively affected the supply of movies. Telang and Waldfogel found that piracy had a negative effect on the number of movies and their quality.

Telang and Waldfogel did not measure the effect of piracy on the US film market over the same time period. They could not identify a clear measurable moment when piracy suddenly affected US profits. Americans still enjoy going to the movies and are willing to pay services like Netflix or cable companies for online access, so clear "before" and "after" piracy time periods were harder to find. Not surprisingly, the effect of piracy in India from 1985 to 2000 was finally blunted by the emergence of multiplex cinemas that drew Indian viewers away from pirated videos. The sensitivity of the film industry to piracy, therefore, may relate to movie makers' ability to provide a product that online pirates cannot easily replicate, e.g., 3D, large screen, Dolby Sound, and a crowd with whom to share the experience.

SOPA and PIPA

The point of this chapter is not to defend pirates but to suggest that empirical research is necessary to evaluate the precise threat posed by piracy. Understanding the effect of piracy on creativity is critical to evaluating the appropriateness of proposed legislative responses. The data presented in this chapter provide an empirical justification for the opposition to Congress's most famous attempt to address online piracy: the Stop Online Piracy Act (SOPA) [the Senate version was called the Protect IP Act, or PIPA].[8]

In 2011, a proposed House bill to fight rampant piracy was met by overwhelming opposition from consumers and important industry players like Facebook, Yahoo!, Twitter, eBay, Wikipedia, and Google (the last two of which went dark for a day in protest). The key provisions of the proposed legislation aimed at credit card companies that serviced pirate websites and firms advertising on pirate websites. Shutting down pirate sites themselves is virtually impossible, especially when their servers are overseas, so the rationale of the legislation was to cut off the supply of funds to the sites. Without income, the pirate economy would be strangled.

SOPA would have given broad new powers to copyright owners. The bill proposed a new category of website, one "dedicated to the theft of US property," which was defined as "primarily designed or operated for the purpose of [or] that engages in, enables, or facilitates [copyright or TM counterfeiting]." Few objected to targeting websites "primarily designed" to infringe, but the bill's language covered all sites that enabled or facilitated infringement, with no requirement of bad intent. In other words, eBay and YouTube were both clearly sites "dedicated to the theft of US property." Why? Because many people sell counterfeit goods on eBay. After all, how can eBay tell whether someone is selling a genuine Tiffany brooch or a fake one? Of course, this book has already detailed the high level of unauthorized uploading on YouTube.

Next, SOPA would have given powerful new rights to copyright owners to suffocate sites "dedicated to the theft of US property." On the basis of a mere good-faith belief that a site was so "dedicated," copyright owners could demand payment service providers (banks, PayPal, credit card companies) and advertisers to stop doing business with the site within five days. If not, the payment provider or advertiser would be liable for damages. To further encourage compliance, the bill provided immunity for payment providers and advertisers who complied with blanket cease-and-desist demands, regardless of whether the sites they serviced actually violated the law.

If the legislation had passed, advertisers would have had five days to abandon YouTube, striking it a crippling blow, and eBay would have lost its ability to transfer funds from buyers to sellers, essentially destroying the site. It's not hard to imagine how other popular sites, like Facebook, would have been devastated.

Despite bipartisan support in Congress and pressure from the Recording Industry Association of America (the main lobbying group for record companies), the US Chamber of Congress, the Better Business Bureau, the AFL-CIO, and other groups, the bill languished and was never brought up for a vote.

Perhaps one does not need data to see the wrongheadedness of the proposed legislation, but it helps to have data showing that rampant piracy did not cripple the music industry.

Moral Rights and Lost Profits

This chapter has taken a highly economic approach, considering the diminishment of creative incentives as the only real threat posed by piracy. The Supreme Court virtually dictates such an approach: "It may seem unfair that much of the fruit of the compiler's labor may be used by others without compensation.

[However], this is not 'some unforeseen byproduct of a statutory scheme.' It is, rather, 'the essence of copyright,' and a constitutional requirement. The primary objective of copyright is not to reward the labor of authors, but 'to promote the Progress of Science and useful Arts.'"[9]

Supreme Court pronouncements aside, some readers (especially Europeans) are distressed whenever an author loses control over a work or when profits tumble. Those taking a "moral" approach to copyright may be offended by Lunney's blunt (but legally correct) statement: "The purpose of copyright is not to maximize the revenue of the music industry, or copyright owners, more generally."[10]

As discussed earlier in this chapter, one could take the position that a user must always ask permission before copying and that piracy should be discouraged at all costs to maintain the author's control over a work. Copyright law could be more protective of authors and less solicitous of consumers and follow-on creators. Copyright could focus less on optimizing incentives to create and instead commit to maximizing the wealth of present artists at the expense of consumers and of future artists who would pay higher license fees to build on prior authors' works.

An "authors first" approach is ultimately very difficult to operationalize. Where should the property line be drawn? What is the overriding principle that should drive legislation and court decisions? Should fair use exist at all? If so, how does one determine whether a use is "fair"? To what extent should the law recognize the need for future artists to have sufficient raw materials to create new works?

One could decide issues case by case using some notion of "fairness" or "justice," but my guess is that norms here are unsettled. For example, what moral principle determines whether a future author should have to wait 50 years or 70 years after another author's death to write a sequel to her book or make a new arrangement of her music?

People's instincts differ on these matters. Some argue that morality compels perpetual copyright; others argue that any term extension for existing works is immoral. After all, when George Gershwin wrote "An American in Paris" in 1928, he thought he was getting 56 years of protection in return for his labor. Is it moral to deny the American public the benefit of that bargain struck between Gershwin and Congress—free use in 1984?

Utilitarianism and efficiency are imperfect tools, but one can at least articulate a roughly workable set of standards. Economics cannot always claim the moral high ground, but its rhetoric—even when startling—has provided a usable framework for more than 200 years.

Can't we agree that giving public welfare as much weight as artists' rights contains a significant moral component?

CHAPTER NINE

GRAY MARKETS AND THE ENTERPRISING MR. KIRTSAENG

I HATE TO ADMIT IT, but some problems are insoluble, even with powerful empirical tools. For example, neither law nor economics can provide a definitive answer to the simple question of when a copyright owner should have the power to stop noninfringing goods at the US border.

Imagine J. K. Rowling writes a new Harry Potter book. Consistent with her prior practice, she would like the UK version to come out before the US version (which always contain variant spellings of English words). If a UK infringer copies the book illegally and seeks to import it into the US, Rowling will be able to stop the shipment of counterfeits at the US border. But what if a clever entrepreneur buys hundreds of legitimate versions of the book from UK bookstores to sell them in the US, presumably for a premium price given the inevitable high demand and lack of supply before the official US launch? Should Rowling be able to prevent the arbitrager from doing so?

Rowling might use contract law to attempt to prevent legitimate UK copies from leaking across the US border. Economists label legal copies that cross borders over the objection of an intellectual property (IP) owner as "gray market goods." Rowling could, for example, make UK booksellers promise not to sell in the US, but how can a bookstore control what its customers do with the books they buy?

Rowling would like to use copyright law as a shield at the US border. This power, widely sought by the most powerful owners of copyrights, patents, and trademarks, poses one of the thorniest economic issues in all of IP law.

The crux of the problem can be captured in three compelling stories.

The Enterprising Mr. Kirtsaeng

Supap Kirtsaeng came to the US from Thailand to study math at Cornell University.[1] Like many students, he was struck by the high price of his textbooks, especially since he knew that the same books sold for much less in Thailand. A lightbulb lit up over his head, and he began asking friends and relatives to buy textbooks back home and ship them to him in the US. He not only obtained copies for his personal use but took advantage of the price difference to make more than $1 million in gross revenue by selling the books on platforms like eBay. Major publisher John Wiley & Sons eventually sued Kirtsaeng, and his case went all the way to the US Supreme Court (more on that later).

Clear winners from Kirtsaeng's scheme were his US buyers, who were able to purchase cheaper textbooks. Wiley & Sons was clearly a loser, given that it lost potential sales to Kirtsaeng's buyers. Less obviously, Thai consumers were also potential losers, given that Wiley's likely response to Kirtsaeng (and others like him) would be to raise prices in Thailand or withdraw from that market altogether to prevent arbitrage and protect the more profitable US market. From an economic perspective, how should Wiley's case against Kirtsaeng come out?

On the one hand, economists usually advocate free trade. Economists generally hate restraints at borders that stop the free flow of goods. An emphasis on free trade favors Kirtsaeng and US consumers. On the other hand, economists also love price discrimination, the notion that producers should sell goods at different prices to different consumers based on their willingness to pay. Thai book buyers are poorer than their US counterparts; they cannot afford to pay a high American price. Wiley, however, is willing to make a smaller profit by selling to them at a lower price. Fostering this sort of price discrimination is, like free trade, a foundational tenant of free market economics.

AIDS Drugs in Africa

Humanitarians have cheered price discrimination when AIDS drugs are sold in Africa. The treatment of AIDS in the US and EU is expensive, as pharmaceutical companies seek to recoup the high cost of drug research, development, testing, and regulatory approval. Manufacturing the drugs is not terribly expensive—even sold at a low price, they generate a profit. So, the natural business plan for pharmaceutical companies is to charge much higher prices in wealthier countries than in poorer countries. Initially, however, international pharmaceutical companies were unwilling to sell AIDS drugs cheaply in Africa. They were worried about entrepreneurs, like Kirtsaeng, who could purchase the drugs cheaply there and then reimport them into the US and Europe, thereby eroding sales and frustrating the recovery of the cost of bringing the drug to the market in the first place.

Not surprisingly, most observers preferred to see price discrimination prevail over free trade. The World Trade Organization responded positively by changing its rules involving the compulsory licensing of patented drugs. It acknowledged pharmaceutical concerns by requiring strict packaging rules to reduce the possibility of AIDS drug arbitrage. Drug companies, with the help of various non-profits, eventually dropped the price of their treatments and greatly increased the availability of critical AIDS drugs. From 2002 to 2012, access to AIDS drugs increased a hundredfold in sub-Saharan Africa. "Expanded treatment access in sub-Saharan Africa is due, in part, to a major drop in the cost of HIV treatment regimens. In 2000, the cost of a year's supply of first-line HIV treatment was about US$10,000 per person; today, it is less than $100 per person."[2]

Omega Watches in Costco

The African AIDS story suggests strongly that at least one group of IP owners should have control at the border to maintain international price discrimination. Not all stories, however, are so heartwarming.

Omega is a Swiss watch company that sells through a series of exclusive distributors.[3] When US watch retailers not authorized to sell Omega watches discovered that Omega was selling its products more cheaply overseas, they began an import and resale program much like Kirtsaeng's. Omega's response was quite tricky. It etched a tiny globe on the back of each of its watches and claimed that, as the copyright owner in the etching, it had the right to stop Costco from importing the watches into the US.

Omega used copyright as a means to frustrate the free flow of goods into the US, and one is hard-pressed to articulate a humanitarian reason justifying the substantial difference between the US and overseas prices of the watches at issue. Omega looked like a monopolist gouging US consumers and hiding behind copyright doctrine to maintain an anticompetitive position.

Gray Market Goods as a Legal Issue

Everyone agrees that IP owners should be able to stop the importation of infringing goods. Indeed, international law requires it, but no treaty compels any jurisdiction to either ban or welcome noninfringing, noncounterfeit goods at its border.[4] Neither law nor economic theory provides a clear answer to the question, so each country is free make its own choice. For example, if a copyright owner in the EU has authorized the sale of a copy of a work in any EU country, that particular copy may freely travel across the border of any EU country, even if the copyright owner objects. However, if the item was first sold *outside* the EU, then the IP owner can prevent its importation into any country of the EU. So, John Wiley & Sons can prevent Kirtsaeng from buying Wiley textbooks in Thailand and importing them into the EU without Wiley's permission. However, books sold first by Wiley in the EU move freely from state to state.

US law is less straightforward. Section 602(a)(1) of the Copyright Act applies to the importation of books, paintings, CDs, DVDs, sheet music, sculptures, and so on. It also applies to any item bearing original artwork, which is a huge category of products given the common use of graphic logos and images on consumer goods. Section 602 seems to give very strong border control rights to copyright owners: "[i]mportation into the United States, without the authority of the owner of copyright under this title, of copies . . . of a work that have been acquired outside the United States is an infringement of the exclusive right to distribute copies . . . under section 106."

The reference to section 106 of the Copyright Act, however, causes trouble for copyright owners because it references section 109, which states that "the owner of a particular copy or phonorecord lawfully made under this title . . . is entitled, without the authority of the copyright owner, to sell or otherwise dispose of the possession of that copy." In other words, once a copyright owner has sold a good, the buyer can resell that good without restriction. This "first sale" doctrine is why we have used book and video game stores, flea markets, and eBay, despite the fact that IP owners hate having to compete with used versions of their goods (which inevitably undercut the price of new goods). Under section 109, it looked at first like Kirtsaeng's business model was legal, as long as the Wiley books he bought in Thailand were originally made and sold by Wiley.

Kirtsaeng, however, lost in the US Court of Appeals for the Second Circuit. That influential court (which covers New York, Connecticut, and Vermont) held that the freedom to transfer goods "lawfully made under this title" meant "goods made in the USA."[5] Since the Wiley books bought by Kirtsaeng were manufactured overseas, he was initially found guilty of copyright infringement due to his unauthorized importation. The mammoth Ninth Circuit (California, Oregon, Washington, Alaska, Idaho, Montana, Arizona, Nevada, and Hawaii) took the same position, and when the case went to the Supreme Court in 2013, the Solicitor General of the United States (representing the Obama administration) wrote a brief urging affirmance of the judgment against Kirtsaeng.

Justice Breyer, speaking for a unanimous Court, disagreed and found for Kirtsaeng. First of all, he noted that "lawfully made under this title" language did not contain any geographical limitations. The phrase just meant "noninfringing" (like the books bought by Kirtsaeng). Moreover, a holding against Kirtsaeng greatly threatened the flow of commerce into the US. Breyer pointed out that "[a] geographical interpretation would prevent the resale of, say, a car, without the permission of the holder of each copyright on each piece of copyrighted automobile software."[6] Can you imagine a phalanx of software programmers standing at the border stopping the flow of Japanese and German cars into the US? Detroit automakers might cheer, but the Court doubted Congress planned such a result when it passed section 109. The justices interpreted the right to sell copyrighted goods "lawfully made under this title" as permitting the importation of noninfringing goods, gutting the power of copyright owners.

The Court also seemed very aware of the game playing of those like the Omega watch company seeking to maintain their exclusive US distribution chains: "Retailers tell us that over $2.3 trillion worth of foreign goods were imported in 2011. American retailers buy many of these goods after a first sale abroad. And, many of these items bear, carry, or contain copyrighted 'packaging, logos, labels, and product inserts and instructions."[7] Giving border control to copyright owners posed a massive threat to Target, Costco, Walmart, and other retail firms.

The case seems like an easy win for all sorts of US importers, but let's return to the earlier scenario of the new Harry Potter book. Imagine, realistically, that Rowling first negotiates with Scholastic Books, to whom she sells her US copyright (but only her US rights). Then, she contracts with Booming Press, an independent UK publishing house to whom she sells her UK rights. Booming is an efficient and hungry press that quickly makes the new book available on the UK market. Its books begin to flood into the US, much to the annoyance of Scholastic, which was slow to fire up its presses. Scholastic argues that importation of the Booming edition should cease. This hypothetical situation raises the issue of whether authors and publishing houses are still able to divide up markets, as they did prior to *Kirtsaeng*.

At first glance, it looks like Scholastic has little chance of stopping the Booming books at the US border. After all, in *Kirtsaeng*, the Supreme Court held that the location of the manufacturer of the books was irrelevant. A first sale *anywhere* of a work "lawfully made under this title [the Copyright Act]" exhausted all the copyright owner's border rights. Is there an argument that the UK Harry Potter books made by Booming were not "lawfully made under this title"? Booming had a valid contract with Rowling, after all. It's not a pirate selling counterfeit copies that a US copyright owner can easily stop at the border.

On the other hand, Scholastic has a plausible argument to stop importation of the Booming edition. It can't argue that the books weren't "lawfully made," but Scholastic might claim they were not "made under this title." The Booming books were made in the UK by a UK copyright owner. Booming has no rights under US law. Far from it! Scholastic was the only party with rights under US law. The books printed by Booming were not made with the permission of the US copyright owner. Rowling no longer owned the US copyright when she contracted with Booming. The Booming books were not made unlawfully; however, they were not printed and sold under US law. Most important, they were made without permission of the US copyright owner.

No cases provide a clear answer to this hypothetical, but the argument in favor of Scholastic does not violate any language found in *Kirtsaeng*, and giving rights to copyright owners in this context would dovetail with the way US law deals with trademark owners who want to bar goods at the border.

Conclusion

Despite the usefulness of economic theory and empirical data in cracking some of the most difficult questions in copyright law, they help little in figuring out how to regulate IP rights at national borders. As we now know, EU importation restrictions are the opposite of US rules for copyrights. Both jurisdictions presumably want to maximize the wealth of their citizens; yet, they come to radically different conclusions on how to accomplish that goal at the border.

If the best economists and brightest politicians in the world can't agree, then I give up.

CHAPTER TEN

MUSIC IN MOVIES

BEFORE CONCLUDING with an analysis of the Supreme Court's most important recent copyright decision, let's take a quick trip to the movies to set up a key question addressed in that case: do bad things happen when works fall into the public domain? Politicians, lobbyists, and trade negotiators have answered yes when advocating for extended terms of protection for copyrighted works. They offer three main arguments.

1. When a work falls into the public domain, that work will be less likely to be exploited because it no longer has an owner to champion it (underexploitation hypothesis).
2. When a work falls into the public domain and becomes free for anyone to use, it will be overused and worn out (overexploitation hypothesis). Yes, this argument contradicts the first argument.
3. If a work falls into the public domain and no longer has an owner to monitor its use, it will become subject to degrading and tarnishing uses that erode its value (debasement hypothesis).

Previous chapters have cast doubt on these hypotheses, but we can make a fuller response after examining what happens to songs when they enter the public domain.

My first thought was to measure whether songs were played more or less frequently on the radio after they entered the public domain, but unfortunately, ASCAP won't share its data. Tracking the sale of CDs or iTunes downloads before and after the copyright in a musical composition expires would also be interesting, but historical data are not publicly available. Each music publishing company keeps its own records, and sales data for individual song titles are not aggregated by any single entity.[1]

Fortunately, data about movies, and more important, the use of songs in movies, are available through websites like IMDB.com and boxofficemojo.com. The openness of these two databases makes it possible to measure the frequency songs appear in movies after the songs enter the public domain.

Are Songs Underexploited in Movies after They Fall into the Public Domain?

Two prominent economists, one of whom is also a well-known federal judge, both worry that "the absence of copyright protection for intangible works may lead to inefficiencies because of impaired incentives to invest in maintaining and exploiting these works."[2] This is the underexploitation thesis in a nutshell: when a work (like a song) falls into the public domain, no one has the exclusive right to exploit it. Without the incentives provided by exclusivity, the work will be neglected.

As applied to the use of songs in movies, the prediction is that when a song enters the public domain, it will be less likely to appear in a film. I find this counterintuitive, given that a filmmaker can save a licensing fee by using a public domain song.

Take, for example, the tear-jerking Irish classic "Danny Boy." Did I say "Irish" classic? The lyrics to "Danny Boy" were actually written by Fredrick Weatherly, a well-heeled Englishman who had never even been to Ireland at the time he penned the song.[3] The lyrics were initially paired with an unremarkable tune until his Irish sister-in-law introduced him to "The Londonderry Aire," a haunting folk tune that better matched his words. The rest is history. It was published in 1913 and became popular at the time millions of young men were perishing in World War I. Played at the funerals of John F. Kennedy and Elvis Presley, and responsible for untold rounds of teary drinking in Irish pubs, it is the most memorable song of the first two decades of the twentieth century.

"Danny Boy" entered the public domain in the US in 1988. In 2009, when I first conducted research on the song in the massive IMDB movie database, I could find no appearances of the song while it was still protected by copyright. Since then, IMDB has continued to add new titles and more data, and "Danny Boy" is now found in at least five pre-1988 movies: *The Road to Happiness* (a 1941 film with John Boles—Shirley Temple's confederate father in *The Littlest Rebel*—singing the song); *Pursued* (a 1947 film with Robert Mitchum singing); *He Laughed Last* (a 1956 film directed by Blake Edwards of *Pink Panther* fame, featuring Frankie Lane singing the song at a mob boss's funeral); *Once Upon a Time in the West* (1968); and—don't ask me why—*Can't Stop the Music* (a 1980 film about the Village People).

Since the copyright on the song expired in 1988, it has appeared in at least 16 movies: *Family Business* (1989) (how could a film with Sean Connery, Dustin Hoffman, and Matthew Broderick be so bad?); *Goodfellas* (1990) (incidental); *Miller's Crossing* (1990) (sung by Frank Patterson, Ireland's "Golden Tenor"); *Memphis Belle* (1990) (with Harry Connick Jr., starring and singing); *When Pigs Fly* (1993) (check out Jackie Wilson's doo-woppy version on YouTube); *Kids* (1995); *The Great White Hype* (1996) (Brian Setzer!); *The Matchmaker* (1997); *The Boxer* (1997); *Good Will Hunting* (1997) (incidental); *Urban Relics* (1998); *The Accountant* (1999); *Return to Me* (2000); *L.I.E.* (2001); *Role Models* (2008); and *12 Rounds* (2009).

We should note that the uptick in use of "Danny Boy" is not due to a preference in the database for newer movies. As of this writing (July 17, 2018), the IMDB database contains 140,274 feature films released between 1930 and 1988, and 175,772 feature films released between 1989 and 2018. Although the number of post-1988 films in the database is 25 percent higher than the number of pre-1988 films, that difference cannot account for the fourfold increase in the number of uses of "Danny Boy" after it fell into the public domain in 1988.

This one anecdote hardly proves that "Danny Boy" appeared in more movies after 1988 *because* it entered the public domain, but it suggests a way to measure what happens to songs in movies once their copyrights expire. Why not take a larger sample of movies and measure the likelihood of a song appearing in a movie before and after it falls into the public domain?

Using Julius Mattfeld's database of the most popular songs in American history,[4] I constructed my own database of 601 songs from 1909 to 1922 that entered the public domain between 1984 and 1997, and 694 songs from 1923 to 1932 that remain under copyright. At the time, under US law, all songs published before 1923 were in the public domain; songs from 1909 to 1922 fell into the public domain 75 years after they were published. The Sonny Bono Term Extension Act of 1998 prevented any songs from falling into the public domain between 1988 and 2018.

A look at the sample reveals an interesting artefact: the songs from 1923 to 1932 are a lot more familiar! This period includes the richest years of Tin Pan Alley and includes songs like "Bye Bye, Blackbird," "Blue Skies [Smiling at Me]," "My Blue Heaven," "Let's Do It [Let's Fall in Love]," "Let's Misbehave," "When You're Smiling—The Whole World Smiles with You," "Bolero," "Happy Days Are Here Again," "Singin' in the Rain," "Star Dust," "Embraceable You," "Georgia on My Mind," "Get Happy," "I Got Rhythm," "Just a Gigolo," and "Mood Indigo." During this time, Cole Porter, the Gershwin brothers, Harold Arlen, Hoagy Carmichael, Duke Ellington, and many others were in the prime of their famous composing careers.

Of 74 songs that appeared in at least four movies by 2009, only 19 were from 1909 to 1922, with the most famous being "Danny Boy," "St. Louis Rag," "Alexander's Ragtime Band," "Over There," and "Colonel Bogey's March" (remember the whistling in *Bridge over the River Kwai*?). The other 55 songs appearing in at least four movies were from the more fertile 1923 to 1932 set of songs.

To control for the effect of popularity, we can measure the change in movie usage of the songs as they transition into the public domain and compare with the changing rate of use of copyrighted songs over the same time period. If we compare the rates of increase, we find the more popular set of a copyrighted song were used at a more slowly increasing rate. Figure 10.1 shows that, on average, a song from 1909 to 1922 appeared in 0.065 movies per year while still protected by copyright, or roughly once every 15.3 years. After those songs fell into the public domain, they appeared 0.263 times per year, or roughly once every 3.8 years. Over the same period, use of songs from 1923 to 1932 also increased, from once every 7.8 years to once every 3.3 years, a slower rate of increase.

To summarize, after falling into the public domain, the songs from 1909 to 1922 appeared in about four times as many movies as when they were protected by copyright, while the songs from 1923 to 1932 appeared in about two and a half times as many films over the same time period. At least for this sample of

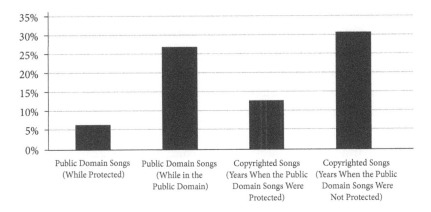

FIGURE 10.1. Average Yearly Use of a Song in a Movie. Source: Paul J. Heald, "Testing the Over- and Under-Exploitation Hypotheses: Bestselling Musical Compositions (1913–32) and Their Use in Cinema (1968–2007)," *Rev. Econ. Res. of Copyright Issues* 6 (2009): 37.

more than 1,200 songs, we cannot see a negative effect associated with public domain status.

We should not, unfortunately, conclude that falling into the public domain necessarily has a *positive* causal effect on song use. My colleagues at the University of Illinois statistical consulting center tell me a phenomenon called the "confounding effect of time" in the data means the only conclusion we can confidently claim is that entering the public domain had no *negative* effect on song use, which does, at least, counter the key underexploitation claim made by copyright term extension enthusiasts.

To further investigate my initial findings, the most frequently used songs were analyzed in terms of the box office data for the films in which they appeared. After all, if the public domain songs all appeared in obscure art-house films and the copyrighted songs all appeared in blockbusters, then there might be a negative effect on overall listening associated with the public domain.

Once again, we found that being in the public domain did not make songs less attractive targets for movie producers. While they were still protected by copyright, the most popular of the public domain songs (those appearing in at least four movies) were in movies with a combined gross of more than $384 million, about $20 million per song. After they fell into the public domain, they were heard in films with a combined gross of almost $4 billion, or about $131 million per song, a sixfold increase. The box office gross for the copyrighted songs also increased, but not as much: from $70 million per song to $141 million per song. Once again, my statistics colleagues could not confidently tell me that we observed a positive public domain causal effect. However, and just as important for the debate, no negative effect was associated with the public domain.

Having seen statistically positive public domain effect in book markets, it was a little disappointing to conclude merely that public domain status does no harm to songs, but perhaps the conclusion is not surprising. The choice of a public domain song really doesn't save the movie producer massive amounts of money. Sure, a licensing fee is saved, but in the context of a huge movie budget, the marginal savings might not stimulate producers to prefer the public domain.

Songs in 100 Famous Movies

Changing methodology, we took a close look at the top 100 grossing movies of all time (fig. 10.2). We calculated the age of each song at the time of the movie's release to see how frequently producers of successful movies included public domain songs in their soundtracks. The task was complicated by the fact that until 1978, the maximum term of copyright in the US was 56 years. In 1978, Congress increased the term to 75 years for existing works, and in 1998 extended it to 95 years. So, depending on the movie release date, the reservoir of public domain songs was a moving target.

Not surprisingly, about half the songs in the films were recorded within one year of the film's release. Many films take place in the present day, and producers logically prefer to include mostly contemporaneous music. In general, the older the song, the less likely it was to be in a movie, except at the bump in the chart associated with the use of public domain songs. The circled portion contains the most telling part of the graph. Due to twentieth-century term extensions, some 60- and 70-year-old songs in the study were in the public domain at the time of the movie release, while other 60- and 70-year old songs were protected by copyright when the movie was released. The public domain subset were significantly more likely to be used by producers than copyrighted songs of the same age.

Combined with the earlier data presented on books, the music-in-movies studies cast serious doubt on the underexploitation hypothesis.

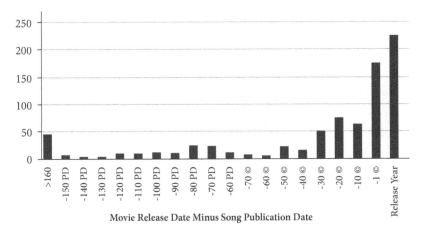

FIGURE 10.2. Songs from Top 100 Grossing Films. Source: Paul J. Heald, "Testing the Over- and Under-Exploitation Hypotheses: Bestselling Musical Compositions (1913–32) and Their Use in Cinema (1968–2007)," *Rev. Econ. Res. of Copyright Issues* 6 (2009): 37.

But Maybe There's Overexploitation

Is it possible that the free availability of public domain works will result in their overuse, causing the public to tire of them and reducing their value?

Considering music-in-movies is a good place to find answers. First, consider the likely behavior of copyright owners. Copyright owners can control how often their songs are used and have a strong profit motive to prevent overuse. The data discussed above showed that on average copyright owners were willing to license their songs in movies about once every 3.3 years. The public domain songs appeared in movies only once every 3.8 years, making it very difficult to argue that the public domain causes levels of use beyond which a rational copyright owner would tolerate.

Looking at the licensing patterns of individual songs is also instructive. The owners of the most popular copyrighted songs were happy to license their use at rates much higher than once every 3.3 years. During the 1930s, "Sweet Georgia Brown" (1925) (the Harlem Globetrotters' theme music) appeared in 15 movies. Harry Akst and Grant Clarke published "Am I Blue" in 1929, and it appeared in 17 movies in the 1930s. The champion for that decade, however, is "Happy Days Are Here Again" (1929), which appeared in 34 movies. More recently, Hoagy Carmichael's "Stardust" (1929), Irving Berlin's "Blue Skies" (1926), and

Gus Kahn's "Dream a Little Dream of Me" (1931) each appeared in 10 films during the 1990s and early 2000s.

The most intensively used public domain songs were "Danny Boy" (1913), with 9 film appearances between 1993 and 2001, and "After You've Gone" (1918), with 9 film appearances between 1996 and 2006. Notably, the frequency of use of the most commonly used public domain songs is the same or lower than that of the copyrighted songs. Overexploitation of songs does not seem to be a problem in the movies.

In general, it seems a bit silly to worry about the overexploitation of songs when the American Society of Composers and Publishers (ASCAP) seems utterly untroubled by the possibility. ASCAP is in charge of licensing the largest single US repertoire of music to radio stations, streaming services, music venues, bars, sports arenas, retail stores, skating rinks, and virtually any other place you are likely to hear music. The standard licensing contract does not limit the number of times a licensee can play a song in the ASCAP catalog. On one day during the 2016 winter break, the University of Georgia's student-run radio station, WUOG 90.5 FM, continually looped Eerie Wanda's throbbin' and groovin' "Volcano Lagoon" all afternoon. No problem! ASCAP could easily insert a limitation-on-play clause in its licensing agreements, but it takes no steps to prevent any licensee from "overexploiting" its songs.

ASCAP is not stupid. Why would a radio station (WUOG aside) want to annoy its listeners by overplaying a song? Why would a bar or restaurant want to lose patrons by overplaying a song? Or a skating rink? ASCAP rationally relies on its licensees' business sense and profit motivations to reduce the potential threat of overexploitation.

Does that mean we, the consuming public, are never annoyed by the songs we hear on the radio or in businesses? Of course we are! As I've already stated, if I hear the "O Fortuna" chorus from *Carmina Burana* once more, I may stick knitting needles in my ears. The fact that *Carmina Burana* is still under copyright has hardly prevented the devaluation of that work to me.[5]

In fact, because only a small percentage of the music you hear on commercial radio or in retail stores is in the public domain, chances are that you are being annoyed by copyrighted songs. If the owners of those works do nothing to prevent overuse, why should Congress enlarge their rights?

Tarnishment of Public Domain Songs

Remember tarnishment from chapter 4? It's the worry that an inappropriate use of a work will debase it, prompting a public reaction so negative that the work's value is reduced. To return to a previous example, a movie could be so terrible that viewers lose interest in reading the book on which it is based.

In general, I expect that the good business sense of those who purvey works to the public should prevent most tarnishment. Let's say a new recording of a classic song is so terrible that listeners don't want to hear any other version of it. Should this fear justify a new copyright term extension so that the song always has an owner to protect it? But think a moment: How would you ever encounter the debasing song in the first place? No one would be interested in advertising and selling it. No business would want it as background music. It might find a home on a quiet corner of YouTube, but you'd never have to listen to it. In other words, the market should police a lot of debasing uses.

But that's jumping the gun. We really need to think harder about what values tarnishment or debasement theory could be designed to protect. Sticking with music examples makes it easier to see how several harms might be at issue:

1. The harm caused by debasement might be a diminishment in the value of a song. In other words, debasement occurs when consumer demand declines due to a damaging use and total income is reduced to its owner.

2. The harm might be a net loss in public welfare, as opposed to the private loss an owner might suffer. Importantly, if adequate substitutes exist for a song whose value is destroyed, then consumers suffer no net loss of welfare. For example, if listeners hear 10,000 fewer streams of a song after an inappropriate use, but hear instead 10,000 more streams of equally good songs, then they suffer no net loss in welfare.

3. The harm might be psychological damage caused to the songwriter. We could include this harm in measuring the net effect on overall welfare, but advocates of moral rights for artists argue that the creator's right to control takes precedence over net public welfare.

4. The harm might be the "recoding" (changing) of the settled cultural meaning of the song. Again, this harm might be cast in public welfare terms, but some commentators suggest that the original meaning of a

classic work should be preserved, even if subsequent changes in meaning might be welfare-enhancing.[6] We might include in this category harm to listeners who don't like the meanings of their favorite songs subverted, like "We Shall Overcome" being sung at a Klan rally.

As for the first two definitions, the Supreme Court states clearly that the purpose of copyright is to increase net public welfare, not purely private gain: "The primary objective of copyright is not to reward the labor of authors, but 'to promote the Progress of Science and useful Arts.'" Those worried about debasement need to argue that granting copyright owners broader rights will enhance public welfare.

But what about the third rationale, protecting artists' feelings? Obviously, the Supreme Court's utilitarian bent militates against preferring a single artist's emotional welfare over the general public interest in having an accessible public domain. Even when we acknowledge that a song could be used to offend its author, copyright already gives an author the right to control works for her whole life (plus 70 years) for post-1978 works and 95 years for pre-1978 works). And, needless to say, all authors of pre-1923, public domain, songs are dead: they have no feelings left to offend.

Of course, most songwriters transfer their copyrights to music publishers. This is why you sometimes hear a composer complaining futilely that his or her publisher has licensed a song for use by a political party the composer finds offensive.[7] Expanding the scope of copyright for existing works usually benefits publishers, not artists seeking greater control over their works.

Finally, what about uses that "recode" the meaning of a work, destabilize its cultural meaning, and disrupt the public (as opposed to offending the artist). Let's take "Danny Boy" as an example. It currently has strong association with Irish Americans in particular and funerary emotions in general. What if a Mexican rapper, backed up by a Mariachi band, recorded a bouncy Latin dance version of the song? Might this new recording change the meaning of "Danny Boy"? Should we care if Irish Americans don't like hearing the new recording? Would we be more worried if the American Nazi Party adopted "America, the Beautiful" (1910) as its anthem?

We can imagine other ways that a song might be used "inappropriately," in a way that might subvert settled meanings and/or offend loyal listeners. Moreover, we can imagine artwork suffering the same indignities, whether it be a moustache on the Mona Lisa or feces painted on a religious symbol. Even the meaning of a dramatic work could potentially be recoded. Imagine a French existentialist philosopher cannibalizing Aeschylus' immortal trilogy of plays known as the *Oresteia*. Oh wait, Jean-Paul Sartre already did that with *The Flies* (1943), one of the greatest dramatic works of the twentieth century.

Having just tipped my hand, let's double down with Mickey Mouse. If Mickey fell into the public domain, ISIS could adopt a new battle flag showing Mickey beheading an infidel (or Mickey being beheaded). If an offended Mickey fan filed suit against ISIS, the suit would be dismissed immediately on First Amendment grounds. Attempts to "recode" iconic works are generally protected by the First Amendment. The right to offend one's fellow Americans is deeply ingrained in our constitutional order. Therefore, using copyright law to control offensive speech raises some red flags. Copyright law is meant to stimulate new creations, not to give publishers a stealthy power to subvert First Amendment values.

Most important, do we really think that debasement ever actually happens? The data in chapters 4 and 5 show that music parodies do not harm the song targeted in the parody, nor are copyrighted movies tarnished by sexual imagery and innuendo. Not to mention this chapter's suggestion how good business sense prevents many disturbing, unsettling uses. Finally, if you are a University of Chicago–style, hardcore economist, you applaud the notion that we should have competition for cultural meaning in the same way we have competition for the best taco or electric car.

Given the American commitment to free speech and the implausibility of most debasement concerns, granting extra terms of protection to all copyrighted works (millions upon millions of them), as Congress did in 1998, seems like massive and inappropriate overkill.

But was it unconstitutional?

CHAPTER ELEVEN

THE TALE OF THE CHURCH CHOIR DIRECTOR, ERIC ELDRED, AND RBG

INTERNET GURU, constitutional law scholar, fighter of political corruption, and one-time presidential candidate, Professor Lawrence Lessig visited the University of Georgia School of Law in 1999 to give a public lecture. He had been a year behind me in law school thirteen years earlier, so I asked to sit next to him during the pre-lecture dinner. We had a lot to talk about. We were both fuming over the 1998 Sonny Bono Copyright Term Extension Act (CTEA), which had added 20 extra years of protection to existing and future copyrights, effectively freezing the public domain for the next two decades. He had already drafted a complaint and was ready to file a lawsuit challenging the constitutionality of the law. I had read the proposed filing and commented that he might have some problems with the "standing" of his chosen plaintiffs.

To attack a piece of legislation, a plaintiff in federal court must allege that he has suffered, or is about to suffer, a concrete injury caused by the challenged law. This allegation establishes "standing" to sue. The injuries of some of Lessig's proposed plaintiffs seemed rather speculative to me.

"You need more people like my wife," I explained, "a choir director who sits and waits for the stroke of midnight on December 31 every year for a new crop of old choral works to fall into the public domain." He seemed interested, so I continued. "Jill has a tiny yearly music budget at St. Gregory the Great Episcopal Church, about $500, which doesn't buy a lot of new sheet music, so she relies heavily on photocopying public domain scores. Most of what we sing is public domain stuff, and a whole bunch of juicy Ralph Vaughn Williams's pieces would be falling into her lap but for the term extension. She, and the church, have suffered a very tangible injury from the new law."

"Alright," he replied eagerly, "I'll make her a plaintiff."

"Uh, okay . . . "

And so he did.

Although Jill's situation was pretty compelling, Larry found an even better story in the form of Eric Eldred, who ran a website that made public domain texts available in formats more readily accessible to sight-challenged patrons. Like Jill, his business model relied on the flow of works entering the public domain every year. His website was squarely and attractively in the public interest, and he was clearly harmed by CTEA's 20-year moratorium on works entering the public domain.

Sonny Bono's Lasting Impact

The 1998 term extension law was named after entertainer Salvatore Philip ("Sonny") Bono, who had a remarkable career as a songwriter, singer (with his second wife, Cher), television star (also with Cher, including stints before and after their divorce), and as a politician. When his show business career slowed down, Bono was elected mayor of Palm Springs, California, and then served in the US Congress from 1995–98, until his untimely death in a skiing accident at Heavenly Ski Resort in Nevada. He championed copyright term extension, but the eventual legislation passed after his death was officially co-sponsored by his fourth wife, Mary Bono.

Conventional wisdom holds that the 20-year extension was driven by Disney's desire to keep Mickey Mouse from falling into the public domain.[1] Stories reported donations made by Disney to key legislators,[2] but in reality, Congress needed no bribing to get on board with an extension of copyright law. Many, many influential players in the entertainment industry favored the extension. And why not? A change in the law would mean 20 more years of royalties to be collected on popular works published after 1923.

Consider the very short selection of titles given in table 11.1 that would have fallen into the public domain between 1998 and 2008 but for CTEA. In 1998, these works, and many others, were still earning significant royalties. Their owners had every incentive to ask Congress to keep the money flowing an extra 20 years. And, best of all, in return for the continuing income stream, the owners would have to do nothing except a bit of lobbying.

Donkeys and Elephants Singing Kumbayah

Public opposition to the term extension was muted because the harm it caused was diffuse. The continuing royalties were mostly paid by television stations, cable companies, radio stations, record labels, publishing houses, and movie theater chains that could invisibly pass their marginal costs on to consumers. Some academics, including seven Noble Prize–winning economists, filed objections with Congress, but their comments were ignored by the relevant committee. None of the data presented in this book had yet been collected, so mounting an empirical attack on the extension was not an option.

Both liberals and conservatives were on board with CTEA. Democrats are traditional allies of the music, film, and publishing industries who lobbied for the change. Republicans undoubtedly found the strengthening of private property rights appealing. The legislation was so popular that it passed by voice vote.[3] Only one member of the Judiciary Committee objected: "I thought it was a moral outrage," said Hank Brown, a former Colorado senator. "There wasn't anyone speaking out for the public interest."[4]

Once Lessig's lawsuit worked its way to the Supreme Court, liberals and conservatives again found common cause. Overturning the term extension held no appeal for the conservative justices. By passing CTEA, Congress had strengthened property rights held primarily by large corporate owners. A small band of academics whining about the public interest was not going to affect their votes. More important, they saw a grave danger presented by Lessig's argument that language in article 1, section 8, clause 8 of the Constitution was controlling.

TABLE 11.1. Works Prevented from Falling into the Public Domain, 1988–2018.

BOOKS	F. Scott Fitzgerald, *The Great Gatsby* (1925)
	Ernest Hemingway, *The Sun Also Rises* (1926)
	A.A. Milne, *Winnie-the-Pooh* (1926)
	Ernest Hemingway, *A Farewell to Arms* (1929)
	Erich Marie Remarque, *All Quiet on the Western Front* (1929)
	Dashiell Hammett, *The Maltese Falcon* (1930)
	Charles Nordoff and James Norman Hall, *Mutiny on the Bounty* (1932)
	P. J. Travers, *Mary Poppins* (1934)
	Agatha Christie, *Murder on the Orient Express* (1934)
	Margaret Mitchell, *Gone with the Wind* (1936)
	John Steinbeck, *Of Mice and Men* (1937)
	John Steinbeck, *The Grapes of Wrath* (1939)
	Ernest Hemingway, *For Whom the Bell Tolls* (1940)
	Richard Wright, *Native Son* (1940)
MUSIC	George Gershwin, "Rhapsody in Blue" (1924)
	Ben Bernie, Maceo Pinkard, and Kenneth Casey, "Sweet Georgia Brown" (1925)
	Ray Henderson and Mort Dixon, "Bye-Bye Blackbird" (1926)
	Hoagy Carmichel, "Stardust" (1927)
	Irving Berlin, "Puttin' on the Ritz" (1927)
	Bertold Brecht and Kurt Weill, "Mack the Knife" (1928)
	Arthur Freed and Nacio Brown, "Singin' in the Rain" (1929)
	Leonello Casucci and Julius Brammer, "Just a Gigolo" (1929)
	Edward Heyman, Robert Sour, Frank Eyton, and Johnny Green, "Body and Soul" (1930)
	Duke Ellington, Barney Bigard, and Irving Mills, "Mood Indigo" (1931)
	Harold Arlen and Ted Koehler, "Stormy Weather" (1933)
	Jerome Kern and Otto Harbach, "Smoke Gets in Your Eyes" (1933)
	Cole Porter, "Begin the Beguine" (1935)
	Harold Arlen and Yip Harburg, "Over the Rainbow" (1939)
	Glenn Miller, "Moonlight Serenade" (1939)
	Abel Meeropol, "Strange Fruit" (1939)
	Glenn Miller, "In the Mood" (1940)
	Irving Berlin, "White Christmas" (1942)

TABLE 11.1. (CONT.)

MOVIES	
	Frankenstein (1931)
	Dracula (1931)
	The Mummy (1932)
	A Farewell to Arms (1932)
	Duck Soup (1933)
	King Kong (1933)
	The Thin Man (1934)
	Snow White and the Seven Dwarfs (1934)
	A Night at the Opera (1935)
	Captain Blood (1935)
	Mutiny on the Bounty (1935)
	Captains Courageous (1937)
	Gone with the Wind (1939)
	Goodbye, Mr. Chips (1939)
	The Wizard of Oz (1939)
	Wuthering Heights (1939)
	The Hunchback of Notre Dame (1939)
	The Grapes of Wrath (1940)
	The Philadelphia Story (1940)
	Fantasia (1940)
	Pinocchio (1940)
	Citizen Kane (1941)
	Dumbo (1941)
	Casablanca (1942)
	Bambi (1942)
FICTIONAL CHARACTERS	
	Mickey Mouse (1928)
	Tom and Jerry (1931)
	Dick Tracy (1931)
	Conan the Barbarian (1932)
	Popeye (1933)
	The Lone Ranger (1933)
	The Phantom (1936)
	Donald Duck (1937)
	Pluto (1937)
	Superman (1938)

TABLE 11.1. (CONT.)

Batman (1939)
Goofy (1939)
Flash (1940)
Doc Strange (1940)
Cat Woman (1940)
Green Lantern (1940)
Daredevil (1940)
Captain America (1941)
Aquaman (1941)
Wonder Woman (1941)

Source: Wikipedia.

What Have Guns Got to Do with It?

The key language in the intellectual property clause of article 1, section 8, reads: "Congress shall have the power . . . *to promote the progress of science and useful arts* by securing for limited times to authors and inventors the exclusive right to their respective writings and discoveries." Lessig argued that the "to promote the progress" language clearly required Congress to have a public purpose in mind when protecting the "writings" of "authors." Extending the term of copyright to *existing* works could not possibly "promote the progress of science and useful arts." The works were already created, so CTEA could have no incentive effect. The *private* benefit of the law to copyright owners was easy to see, but what public benefit flowed from forcing consumers to pay an extra 20 years of royalties to copyright holders who were under no obligation to earn their pay by creating something new?

The framers of the Constitution included purposive language like "to promote the progress" only twice in the Constitution. As we've just seen, they told Congress in the copyright clause to pass laws only "to promote the progress of science" (meaning "knowledge" at the time the Constitution was written). We have to go to the Second Amendment of the Bill of Rights to find the only other occasion: "*A well-regulated Militia, being necessary to the security of a free State, the right of the people to keep and bear Arms, shall not be infringed.*" The clause seems to specify a purpose for the right to bear arms: to ensure the existence of a "well-regulated Militia."

If conservatives on the Supreme Court accepted Lessig's argument that Congress was constrained by purposive language like "to promote the progress of science," then they would find it very difficult thereafter to find that the language in the Second Amendment similarly granted the right to bear arms only in relation to a "well-regulated Militia."

Once conservative justices in *Eldred v. Ashcroft* rejected the relevancy of "to promote the progress of science," essentially writing it out of the Constitution, they found it easier to do the same with the "well-regulated Militia" clause.[5] Six years later, in 2008, in *District of Columbia v. Heller*, the Supreme Court found that the "well-regulated Militia, being necessary to the security of a free State" language did nothing to constrain an individual's right to bear arms.[6] To avoid the preamble to the Second Amendment in 2008, the conservative justices in *Heller* had to avoid the preamble to the copyright clause in 2003 when they decided *Eldred v. Ashcroft*.

FDR and Justice Ginsburg

Although dissenting Justices Breyer and Stevens thought that extending the term of existing copyrights was unconstitutional, liberal Justice Ruth Bader Ginsburg authored the opinion upholding CTEA. Her motivations undoubtedly differed from those of her conservative colleagues. Without going into too much detail, history shows how conservative justices struck down much of the progressive legislation passed by Congress during the first term of President Franklin Delano Roosevelt. In fact, conservative "activism" had been going on for decades before FDR, resulting in many federal and state laws being declared unconstitutional. In response, deference to Congress became a byword for Democrats attempting to reengineer the social and economic fabric of the country.

FDR's threat to pack the Court with younger, more liberal justices eventually pressured the Court to uphold a higher percentage of New Deal legislation, but the association of conservative politics with enthusiasm to question congressional action remained. New Dealers were staunchly deferential to Congress, and so were the new, more liberal justices that FDR was able eventually to appoint. Progressive politics gradually became identified with a willingness to let Congress, not the judiciary, manage the US economy.

In short, in *Eldred v. Ashcroft*, Justice Ginsburg was caught between a rock and a hard place. On the one hand, she surely held a progressive commitment to upholding congressional action, but on the other, she probably understood that CTEA was raw special interest politics. If she were troubled by the motivations behind CTEA, she overlooked its flaws to remain faithful to the long-standing New Deal commitment by deferring to Congress. So, Ginsburg and the conservatives, each for their own reasons, held hands and declared CTEA constitutional.

Driven by political motivations, untethered from the facts of the case and the constitutional language, the opinion is, unsurprisingly, one of the most incoherent in modern history.

What the Court Said

We can give short shrift to the portion of CTEA that extended the term of copyright for works not yet created. Between 1978 and CTEA in 1998, the term of copyright for new works was life-of-the-author plus 50 years. CTEA, extended the term to life plus 70. Lessig argued that this extension violated the "limited times" of the intellectual property clause of the Constitution. Article 1, section 8, clause 8 states that Congress cannot legislate an eternal copyright; it may protect writings for only "limited times."

The government responded that life-of-the-author-plus-70 is a limited time. It's a long time, to be sure. If an author writes a book in 2020 at age 30 and lives to be 90 (dying in 2080), the term of copyright protection under CTEA for the book will last 130 years (2150 minus 2020 equals 130). But 130 years is not eternal. It is still "limited."

Lessig, backed by seven Nobel Prize–winning economists, argued that in actuarial terms, 130 years was effectively eternal. Accounting for the time value of money and assuming standard interest rates, their math proved that adding 20 years to an average life-plus-50 term did not significantly increase the present value of the copyright and therefore could not possibly incentivize future creations.

Huh?

The easiest way to see the argument is to go to your bank and ask about buying an annuity that will pay you $100 a month for a long period of time, say, 80 years. Assuming a 4 percent interest rate, you'll need to pay the bank slightly less than $29,000 right now to be guaranteed your $100 a month, 80-year payout. Then, ask the bank how much more you'll have to pay to extend your income stream an extra 20 years, from 80 years to 100 years. How much would a 100-year, $100 a month income stream cost you in today's dollars? Surprise, surprise—you'll only have to pay a little bit more than $29,000 to get 20 extra years of payout.

Once economists and actuaries account for what they refer to as the "time value of money," they agree that increasing the length of distantly future income streams even further into the future doesn't really affect the present value of that income stream. In other words, no rational publisher will pay more for the rights to a book simply because it will potentially earn money for 100 years instead of 80, and therefore no rational author will be incentivized to produce an extra word.

No one, however, was shocked when this fancy math failed to impress the Court. Maybe actuaries and economists perceive long income streams as effectively eternal, but the word "limited" has a clear dictionary meaning, and 100 years or 120 or 130 or 140 years are still, literally, "limited" periods of time.

The Court is often a bit pedantic in this regard. Just ask Anthony "Fat Tony" Salerno, a boss in the Genovese crime family who was charged with racketeering in 1986 (*Fortune* magazine named him "Top Mobster" that year).[7] Having been denied bail, Salerno made a very simple argument to the Supreme Court: the Constitution expressly prohibits a court from charging an "excessive bail." Since the complete denial of bail has the same effect as charging an astronomically high bail, say $100 trillion, it was by definition "excessive." He had a point. A denial of bail is essentially the setting of an infinite bail.

Nah, said the Court. "Excessive bail" means the court charged too much money. Since Salerno wasn't charged a big chunk of change, his rights were not violated.

I think Salerno could have told the seven Nobel Prize–winning economists not to bother with their fancy math.

Extending the Term of Copyright in Existing Works

The Court had a much harder time explaining why adding an extra 20 years of life to existing works, reaching all the way back to 1923, was permissible. The core of the problem for defenders of CTEA was that the extension was purely a gift of taxpayer money to copyright owners. The public would pay 20 extra years of royalties to owners, and, in return, owners would not have to do a thing to earn it. Note this runs counter to normal intellectual property principles: you invent a new widget, and you get a patent. You create an artistic work, and you get a copyright. An inventor or artist does some hard work, and the government provides a reward. *Quid pro quo.* That's how we incentivize new inventions and new works of art.

The works protected by CTEA were already created. The legislation was a massive diversion of income from users to copyright owners, no strings attached.

All right, so the legislation was a gift, not a reward. So what? Congress makes gifts all the time in the form of subsidies. In fact, the government regularly makes grants to artists. The National Endowment for the Arts hopes that funding a year-long writing residency for a poet will result in some good poetry, and it doesn't require all the work by the artist to be done up front.

Congress subsidizes farmers, schools, and oil companies, so why could it not have written some big checks to copyright owners? And, of course, it could have. If Congress had determined, for example, that the additional 20 years of royalties was worth $1 billion to copyright owners like Disney, it could have written them checks instead of extending the copyright term. Subsidies present no constitutional problems, although they can cause political turmoil. Subsidies are visible and hotly debated because fiscal watchdogs can see how directly the money goes from taxpayers to the pockets favored by special interests.

Now you can see why Congress chose to hide the transfer in the guise of copyright reform. Instead of permissibly writing a check to Disney and others, Congress took a different route. It granted 20 years of additional "exclusive rights" to copyright owners. But this approach *does* pose a constitutional problem.

The framers of the Constitution were well aware of the infamous history of the English crown making gifts of exclusive rights to favored courtiers.[8] The most famous case involved the granting of the sole right to sell playing cards to a Groom of the Chamber in the court of Queen Elizabeth I.[9] The beneficiary of the grant did not invent playing cards; he just wanted to make a lot of money by charging people who made and sold them. Dozens of other similarly abusive monopolies were granted for things like brewing beer and making glass for windows, all at the expense of the British public.[10] Printing monopolies were also granted by the crown. Eventually, Parliament, with some exceptions, banned the practice.

It's unlikely the lessons of English history were lost on the founding genera-tion here. Remember the protest on the tea monopoly that took place in Boston Harbor? The framers knew how government grants of exclusive rights could be abused. This awareness is the best explanation for the nearly unique preambular language in the intellectual property clause of the Constitution. Article 1, section 8, clause 8 of the Constitution authorizes congressional grants of copyrights and patents only "to promote the progress of science."

This language logically requires a *quid pro quo*, an exchange between a creator and the government. First, write a book; then, Congress will give you an exclusive right to it. Congress has the power to grant exclusive rights, but, unlike the cor-rupt old English monarchy, it must purchase something in return for the public.

Lessig's argument was fairly straightforward in this regard. Congress can-not act like King James or Queen Elizabeth and just hand out exclusive rights to favored interests. Why else would the Constitution add such an unusual pre-amble to the copyright power?

Twisting in the Wind

In rejecting the *quid pro quo* argument and denying any restrictive power to the "progress of science" language, the Court in *Eldred v. Ashcroft* thrashed about in several different directions. First, it recognized, somewhat awkwardly, that the Court itself had deployed the *quid pro quo* argument in patent cases.[11] Since the power to grant patents and copyrights are contained in the same clause of the Constitution, this posed a problem for the Court, which it solved by finding that patents and copyrights were different. Providing no historical evidence, the Court suggested that the framers may have wanted to require inventors to invent something to earn a patent, but no such requirement of new creation existed when Congress extended the length of copyrights.

Among legal scholars, the sophisticated term for this is "waving a magic wand" over a problem to make it go away.

Rational Review

Second, even if the Court had recognized that Congress was constrained by the "progress of science" language, a powerful interpretive tool was deployed by the Court to insulate CTEA from judicial review. Giving Congress true New

Deal deference, the Court held that if the legislature had a "rational basis" for passing CTEA, then it was constitutional. Rational basis review is the weakest level of scrutiny that the Court gives to a statute. The hurdle is so low that almost all legislation passes the test:

> Under rational basis review, it is "entirely irrelevant" what end the government is actually seeking and statutes can be based on "rational speculation unsupported by evidence or empirical data." Rather, if the court can merely hypothesize a "legitimate" interest served by the challenged action, it will withstand rational basis review. Judges following the Supreme Court's instructions understand themselves to be "obligated to seek out other conceivable reasons for validating" challenged laws if the government is unable to justify its own policies.[12]

Between 1971 and 1996, the Court employed rational basis review in 110 cases and struck down only 10 laws.[13]

The Court finds laws irrational in extreme cases, like *Weinberger v. Wiesenfeld*[14] (striking down a part of the Social Security Act that paid benefits to a surviving widow but not to a widower) or *Stanton v. Stanton*[15] (striking down a Utah law that made the age of majority 18 years for women but 21 for men). Putting history and the unique language of the intellectual property clause aside, the Court found that no special scrutiny of CTEA was merited.

Lessig nonetheless argued that CTEA had no rational basis whatsoever, that it was a gift to special interests unjustified by any public welfare considerations. Unable to muster any incentive-based arguments in response to Lessig's characterization, defenders of the statute offered two justifications for the law.

First, the retroactive addition of 20 years to existing copyrights paralleled the additional 20 years added to future copyrights by CTEA. According to its supporters, Congress thereby evidenced a desire that older and new copyrights be put in "parity" with each other. What "parity" means is unclear, given that the immediate beneficiaries of CTEA—owners of works published from 1923 to 1942—would get a 95-year term (up from 75), while new works would be protected for life-of-the-author-plus-70 (up from life-of-the-author-plus-50). In addition, the Copyright Act provides different terms of protection for works-made-for-hire and also differentiates term length for published versus unpublished works.

If you look hard at the statute, it's difficult to see that Congress cares about "parity" among different categories of copyright owners. Calculating the term length for any particular work is a laborious and complicated process that identifies multiple possible terms based on numerous different factors. If Congress cared about "parity," it wouldn't take me two days of painstaking lecturing to teach my class how to calculate a term of copyright for a particular work.

Remember the many complications regarding ownership caused by the three different regimes covering authors' reversion rights? Here's a brief review: If a work was first published on January 1, 1978, the copyright reverts to the original author in 2013. If the work was first published a day earlier, December 31, 1977, the work reverts at either year 56 or year 75. For works published before 1964, reversion happens in year 28, *if* the author was dead at that time.

Does this give any indication how much Congress really cares about parity?

A second, slightly more plausible justification was offered by supporters of CTEA. Since some countries have reciprocal recognition of copyright terms, adding 20 years of copyright protection in the US would lead to 20 extra years of protection for US authors in some jurisdictions abroad. The foreign income stream would come at the expense of foreign consumers, not US consumers. Congress, therefore, could rationally extend the term in the US to garner this benefit.

The problem with this justification is that Congress did not analyze the costs and benefits of CTEA in this regard. Copyright owners would not benefit in all foreign jurisdictions, but only those that had already moved to life-of-the-author-plus-70, *and* who did not automatically apply that term to foreigners already. So, the law gave no benefit to Americans in countries like Japan, Australia, New Zealand, and South Africa, which applied a maximum term of life-plus-50. Nor did CTEA benefit Americans in countries like Brazil and Mexico, which already applied life-plus-70 or more to all foreign copyright owners. Moreover, even in countries where Americans technically benefited, the legal right to collect foreign royalties is often frustrated by the practicalities of doing so.

In other words, a narrow band of American copyright owners would receive an economic benefit from overseas licensing in some markets, but that benefit was certainly swamped by the huge cost CTEA imposed on American consumers. Is it rational to pass a law that results in American consumers paying x dollars in royalties, so that American copyright owners can earn an extra one-tenth of *x* overseas?

But under rational basis review, Congress does not have to do the math. Under rational basis review, the flimsiest of post hoc justifications will suffice, and the Court concluded that Congress acted rationally in passing CTEA.

What to Do with History

In the most disturbing part of the *Eldred* opinion, the Court repeatedly shored up its justifications for CTEA by reference to "an unbroken congressional practice" of retroactive term extension. Congress had, in fact, passed earlier retroactive term extensions without any complaint from the public. Why shouldn't it be able to do so once again?

Let's begin with the original 1793 Copyright Act, which provided 14 years of protection for existing books, charts, and maps (plus a 14-year renewal period if the author was still around to renew). Isn't this clear evidence that the founding generation was fine with retroactive protection? Didn't the first Congress make a clear gift to copyright owners?

(As a quick aside, remember that we don't automatically defer to the judgment of the first Congress. After all, the case of *Marbury v. Madison* provides a famous example of the Court striking down a law passed by the first Congress, which was full of legislators who participated in the Constitutional Convention.[16])

More important, that first copyright statute, which limited copyright protection to 14 years, may have narrowed property rights, not gifted anyone. Copyright owners may have felt something was taken away rather than given to them. How come? Before the constitutional era in American politics, copyright owners in the US had a strong argument under English colonial law that they had a life-long natural right to their creations. Whether they did was never decided, but copyright owners at the time of the first Congress had a plausible argument that their copyrights should last forever. If so, they would have been dismayed to learn that Congress had just chopped their rights down to a mere 14 years. In other words, the 1793 Copyright Act is poor evidence that the framers of the Constitution approved of Congress making gifts of exclusive rights to special interests.[17]

The Copyright Act of 1831 provided the first occasion where Congress clearly extended the term of protection for existing copyrights. The law did not pluck works out of the public domain, but it added 14 more years of protection to works whose copyrights had not yet expired. It also kept open the possibility of yet another additional 14 years if the author renewed its registration.

In 1909, Congress passed another extension with no strings attached, lengthening the renewal term for nonexpired copyrights to 28 years, while keeping the initial copyright term at 28 years. The maximum potential term length stayed at 56 years until 1962, when Congress initiated a series of legislative actions anticipating the 1976 Act that extended the term to 75 years for all works. Finally, in 1998, CTEA extended the term to 95 years for post-1922 works.

So, Congress retroactively extended protection for existing works four times: in 1831, 1909, 1976, and 1998. The three occasions prior to CETA are the "unbroken congressional practice" to which the Court in *Eldred* referred.

The Relevance of Historical Practice to Interpretation

Now would be a good time to ask, why does post-ratification congressional action have any relevance to the question of constitutional interpretation? Constitutional interpretation is pointedly about divining the intent of the ratifiers of the Constitution in 1789. How does congressional action taken years after ratification bear on what was intended by those who made the Constitution law?

Quick note. Whether we approve of interpreting the Constitution according to its original understanding, discerning that intent is generally what the Supreme Court purports to do when it interprets the document.

So, let's repeat the question: How could Congress's actions in 1831, 1909, and 1976 be relevant to what the ratifiers of the intellectual property clause intended in 1789?

To help answer the question, let's step away from copyright for a minute and think about the North American Free Trade Agreement (NAFTA). The trade treaty was negotiated by the executive branch and signed by the president in 1992. It required substantial implementing legislation that Congress passed in 1993, and those new provisions of US law came into force in 1994. This sounds unobjectionable. Congress passed a series of new laws and the president signed them, just like the Constitution demands, right?

However, one of the most notable constitutional law scholars of his generation, Laurence Tribe, claimed that NAFTA was unconstitutionally implemented.[18]

Article 1 of the Constitution states that all treaties need to be approved by a two-thirds vote of the Senate, and NAFTA was never approved by the Senate. Essentially, Congress and the president had converted a treaty into the law of the land without getting the required Senate approval, using the normal legislative process as a simple bypass.

Tribe's argument seems compelling on its face, until you realize how frequently past Congresses and other presidents have done precisely the same thing. If Tribe was correct, then piles of legislation would be invalidated. On the other hand, why should earlier congressional practice somehow bend our understanding of the clear constitutional mandate of two-thirds Senate approval?

The issue was slippery, so slippery that the Court refused to hear the constitutional challenge brought against NAFTA.

The question is especially fraught because the Court in previous prominent cases had rejected the argument that post-ratification practice should influence its reading of the Constitution. For example, in *INS v. Chadha* the Court struck down a congressional practice known as the legislative veto, whereby one house of Congress was granted the power to unilaterally countermand actions by administrative agencies.[19] The case was decided in 1983, and Congress had passed hundreds of laws containing legislative veto provisions. Congressional practice didn't matter, the Court said. Congress could not bypass the Constitution merely because it had consistently acted unconstitutionally for decades. The legislative veto was unconstitutional regardless of how many times Congress had used it. Historical practice would not bind the Court.

During the Korean War, the Court came to a similar conclusion in the Steel Seizure Case, *Youngstown Sheet & Tube Co. v. Sawyer.*[20] The case was prompted by President Truman's temporary takeover of US steel mills to assure the flow of supplies necessary to fight the Korean War. When his action was challenged in the Supreme Court, he argued that the executive branch had taken similar action many times in the past, and government attorneys set forth a long historical record dating back to the Civil War. The Court was unimpressed. A consistent unconstitutional practice could not amend the Constitution.

All right, we have clearly jumped into very complicated water here! The bottom line is that the Supreme Court has never established a test to help us determine when a long, unbroken historical practice is relevant to interpreting the Constitution and when it is not. My friend Peter Spiro has a nice theory that focuses on how openly the historical practice was debated, challenged, and publicized, and whether the opposition acquiesced.[21] The Court, however, has never made it clear when historical practice matters and when it doesn't.

One thing that everyone agrees on, however, is that the practice must be frequent and consistent, although *Chadha* and *Youngstown Steel* show that frequency alone is not enough.

Here are two final thoughts on the matter. First, the Court missed a tremendous opportunity in *Eldred* to spell out when historical practice counts and when it doesn't. Second, accepting three term extensions over 200 years (1831, 1909, 1976) as a sufficiently long, unbroken congressional practice to justify the 1998 CETA is shockingly unusual.

My colleagues who specialize in constitutional law don't really pay attention to intellectual property cases. When I tell them that the Court in *Eldred* determined that three instances in 200 years constituted "a long, unbroken historical practice" worthy of deference, they think I am lying. They don't believe me—until they read the case and their heads explode.

In any event, in *Eldred*, the primary justification for the Court's ruling was based on congressional practice.

Private Laws and History

The Court relied on one last bit of historical evidence that merits a brief discussion. Throughout history, well-connected individuals have gotten Congress to pass private legislation for their benefit. For example, a prominent refugee scientist from a foreign country might bypass the normal immigration process by having Congress pass a "private bill" declaring her a citizen. Over the years, a number of inventors have convinced Congress to extend the length of their individual patents. These were not blanket extensions applicable to entire classes of inventions, but private actions applicable to discrete patents. The Court referenced these private patent bills to prop up its thin evidence of historical practice in the copyright extension arena.

Two facts plague this argument. First, the passage of a private patent extension does not necessarily indicate that Congress is comfortable with making gifts of exclusive rights to intellectual property owners. In most cases, a true *quid pro quo* is involved. Unlike copyright, patent law allows an inventor to obtain a patent before she has actually produced a new physical item for the public. Once the inventor adequately describes the invention on paper, the Patent Office will issue a patent (if the invention is new, useful, and a sufficient improvement over the prior art).[22] This means that some inventors have insufficient time to ramp up actual production. Because we reward invention early on, commercialization can lag by decades.

So, if a patent owner has a sufficiently difficult time commercializing an invention, she may approach Congress and ask for more time to give the public the benefit of the invention. Imagine a patentee who has finally built a prototype and is seeking financing to build a manufacturing facility. The patentee approaches banks and venture capitalists, but the patent is about to expire, and the financiers are worried that the patentee will soon face competition. Without the promise of exclusivity, the investment looks too risky. With the guarantee of an extended patent period and the potential for extended monopoly profit, the money people would be willing to invest. In this situation, a congressional grant of extra time seems designed to get something new into the public market. It's easy to see a *quid pro quo* for the extension.

Second, these private patent bills are, well, private. They are passed without debate and without any publicity. If we accept the position that congressional action should sometimes influence constitutional interpretation, then surely we want the practice to be visible and subject to vigorous public discussion. We don't want Congress to stealthily influence constitutional interpretation when no one is paying attention.

International Obligations Change Nothing

As the Court floundered in *Eldred*, trying desperately to explain how Congress was constitutionally authorized to make gifts of exclusive rights to copyright owners, it made a point of mentioning US treaty obligations. This book began with a description of how the US convinces its trading partners to adopt a copyright term of life-of-the-author-plus-70 years. These same agreements require each party to add 20 years of protection to existing works. The agreements are reciprocal, committing the US to the same extension strategy, which Congress honored in CTEA.

So, do our treaty commitments give Congress constitutional authorization to tack on 20 extra years of protection to our copyright law?

The answer to this question is made abundantly clear in the interesting case of *Reid v. Covert* where the Court held that "no agreement with a foreign nation can confer power on the Congress . . . which is free from the restraints of the Constitution."[23]

The case involved Clarice Covert, who murdered her husband, an army sergeant stationed in the UK. After wielding a deadly axe, she spent the rest of the night with his corpse before going to his military base the next morning and turning herself in. She had told the base psychiatrist the day before the murder that she was going to explode.

The murder occurred in England, and, in accordance with a treaty between the US and the UK, the case was tried by a military tribunal that found her guilty and sentenced her to life at hard labor. Military trials lack juries, and she eventually appealed on the grounds that her Sixth Amendment right to a jury trial had been violated.

The Court held that the treaty could not trump the Constitution, so she was released and, surprisingly, never retried. Finding information about what happened to her and her three children after she was released is difficult, but an Internet post from someone purporting to be her ex-daughter-in-law claims that "she's been rotting in hell since 1992."[24]

To be fair, the Court in *Eldred* did not hold that treaties can trump the Constitution, but in light of *Reid v. Covert*, its references to treaty obligations to support its argument that Congress behaved rationally should be taken with a grain of salt.

One Final Argument

Years of empirical work have made it easy to pass judgment on one final argument made in favor of copyright term extension—that longer copyright terms will increase the number of works available to the public.[25] You now know that the opposite is true, that CTEA has kept untold numbers of books out of print, preventing new editions from being published.

But Congress had no data when it passed CTEA. Was its blissfully ignorant belief that CTEA would increase access and availability a rational one?

Maybe. Rational basis review does not require much to uphold a law. And if we ignore the constitutional language requiring Congress "to promote the progress of science" when it grants exclusive rights, then maybe we can justify lowering the legislative bar so much that a snake can squirm over it.

CONCLUSION

SUMMING UP

CONCLUSIONS OF NONFICTION BOOKS are not supposed to introduce new substantive material, but one important bit of fallout from *Eldred* emphasizes the overall theme of the book. Data show that the extra years of protection approved by the Court came with a measurable price tag for American consumers. Consider the prices charged by Random House for 96 randomly sampled bound volumes from its Penguin Classics collection (table C.1). The copyrighted books are significantly more expensive, and keeping them in copyright imposes a long-term cost on buyers.

Research in Canadian, UK, and South African book markets confirms similar pricing trends for bound volumes. Worldwide, the price difference between copyrighted e-books and public domain e-books is even more striking. On the Canadian version of Amazon, a sample of Vintage Classics showed that copyrighted digital editions cost on average $12.53 Canadian dollars, while their public domain counterparts cost only $6.76. A comparison of prices on the UK version of Amazon showed an even more dramatic difference, £4.34 for copyrighted volumes and £1.30 for public domain volumes.[1]

Copyright assures all sorts of artists the chance of a fair return for their labor. Without copyright, anyone could copy this book and sell it, driving down my

TABLE C.1. Comparative Prices of Public Domain and Copyrighted Penguin Classics.

FORTY-EIGHT COPYRIGHTED BOOKS:
Average price per book: $14.60
Average length: 310 pages
Average price per page: $.047

FORTY-EIGHT PUBLIC DOMAIN BOOKS:
Average price per book: $11.10
Average length: 374 pages
Average price per page: $.03

Source: Heald, 2008, "Property Rights and the Efficient Exploitation," 1049.

profits and destroying my incentive to create it in the first place. And as fun as this book has been to write, I would not have written it in the absence of any reward!

The logical and wholesome incentive rationale for copyright does not mean, however, that every increase in the scope of protection advances public welfare. The data presented in this book are meant to help the public, as consumers of copyright law, determine when a law is public-minded or when it is just a craven grab by special interests. Unfortunately, we've seen how copyright diminishes the availability of important works to the public and how it raises the cost of books. We've seen copyright create a massive orphan works problem, stymying the use of millions of works whose owners cannot be identified. Confusion over ownership makes it even easier for large publishers to put fraudulent copyright symbols on public domain works. Perhaps most frustrating of all, we've seen how courts judging music copyright infringement cases have disincentivized composers, arrangers, and performers.

The empirical research does illuminate some bright spots. Transferring the ownership of copyrights from big publishers to authors helps bring back some of the missing books from the twentieth century. We see heartening research about the minimal impact rampant online music piracy has had on the production of quality music. Finally, the notice and takedown regime that governs YouTube and other similar platforms has nurtured a vibrant market for cultural goods that had disappeared from view.

Captured by large corporate interests, Congress must be carefully monitored. Americans are already sufficiently cynical about the legislative process to understand the need for vigilance. Hopefully, the data presented here provide a tool to give that vigilance a harder edge.

Oh, and if you simply cannot afford to pay for it and would not have bought it anyway, please copy this book!

NOTES

A Brief Note on Copyright Law and the Purpose of This Book

1. Act of May 31, 1790, § 1, 1 Stat. 124 (providing sole rights to citizen who created an original book or map for a term of 14 years).

2. Feist, Inc. v. Rural Tel. Serv., 499 U.S. 340, 349–50 (1991) (noting the objective of copyright law is to assure authors the right of original expression while promoting others to build upon the work).

3. 17 U.S.C. § 302(a) (2018).

Introduction

1. Dwight Macdonald, "By Cozzens Possessed: A Review of Reviews," Commentary, January 1958, https://www.commentarymagazine.com/articles/by-cozzens-possesseda-review-of-reviews.

2. John W. Aldrige, "Novelist of Power and Privilege," New York Times, July 3, 1983, https://www.nytimes.com/1983/07/03/books/novelist-of-power-and-privilege.html (noting that Macdonald's portrayal of Cozzens as a bigot and sexist was responsible for Cozzens not being taken seriously by liberal intellectuals).

3. "By Love Possessed—(Original Trailer)," Turner Classic Movies, accessed January 29, 2020, http://www.tcm.com/mediaroom/video/155455/By-Love-Possessed-Original-Trailer-.html.

4. Paul J. Heald, "How Copyright Keeps Works Disappeared," Journal of Empirical Legal Studies 18 (2014): 840.

5. "Estimated" because the number of books registered is just a proxy for the number of books actually published. Data on the number of books actually published in the decades before 1950 is not available.

6. Arguments before the Comms. on Patents of the Sen. and the H.R. Conjointly, S. 630 & H.R. 19853 (June 6–9, 1906), 116 (statement of Samuel L. Clemens [Mark Twain]).

7. Brief of George A. Akerlof as Amici Curiae in Support of Petitioners, Eldred v. Ashcroft, 537 U.S. 186 (2003) (No. 01-618) (a 20-year extension of the copyright act does not incentivize innovation).

8. Trans-Pacific Partnership, Feb. 4, 2016, US Trade Representative, https://ustr.gov/trade-agreements/free-trade-agreements/trans-pacific-partnership/tpp-full-text.

9. Memorandum for the US Trade Representative, 82 Fed. Reg. 8497 (Jan. 25, 2017) (withdrawal of the US from the Trans-Pacific Partnership Negotiations and Agreements).

10. Barbara Biasi and Petra Moser, "Effects of Copyright on Science," Vox, May 26, 2018, https://voxeu.org/article/effects-copyrights-science (scientific textbooks originally owned by German scientists decline in price and increase in citation after copyright barriers removed).

11. Letter to TPP negotiating countries, from a coalition of copyrighted material users, Electronic Frontier Foundation, July 9, 2014, https://www.eff.org/files/2014/07/08/copyrightterm_tppletter_print-fnl.pdf.

12. Eric Crampton, "Copyright Dead Rats, Bon Appetit," New Zealand Initiative, February 12, 2016, https://www.nzinitiative.org.nz/reports-and-media/opinion/copyright-dead-rats-bon-appetit/ (discussing copyright protection available to international innovators without the TPP).

13. Crampton, "Copyright Dead Rats."

Chapter One

1. Ben Cosgrove, "Mystery in the Sky: A Legendary Photo (Slowly) Gives Up Its Secrets," Time, September, 18, 2013, http://time.com/3449718/mystery-in-the-sky-a-legendary-photo-slowly-gives-up-its-secrets (discussing the possible identities of the men in the famous photo). Lunch atop a Skyscraper is the title given the photograph by Wikipedia, accessed October 9, 2018, https://en.wikipedia.org/wiki/Lunch_atop_a_Skyscraper.

2. "New York Construction Workers Lunching on a Crossbeam," Getty Images, accessed May 12, 2020, https://www.gettyimages.com/detail/news-photo/while-new-yorks-thousands-rush-to-crowded-restaurants-and-news-photo/515612650?adppopup=true [https://perma.cc/RU9V-9B72].

3. Berne Convention for the Protection of Literary and Artistic Works, September 9, 1886, 828 U.N.T.S. 221 (1972) (as amended); Berne Convention Implementation Act of 1988, 102 Stat. 2853.

4. "Lewis Hine," International Photography Hall of Fame and Museum, accessed May 12, 2020, https://iphf.org/inductees/lewis-hine/.

5. "Hamilton Write Jr. Photographs, circa 1923–1925, 1950–1970," Smithsonian Online Virtual Archives, accessed January 29, 2020, http://sova.si.edu/record/NAA.PhotoLot.76-35.

6. Lunch atop a Skyscraper; see also Tami Ebbets Hahn, "Charles C. Ebbets in 1932 the Day He Took the Famous 'Men on a Beam' Image of 11 Steelworkers Having Lunch above Manhattan," Show and Tell, Collectors Weekly, 2012, https://www.collectorsweekly.com/stories/47536-charles-c-ebbets-in-1932-the-day-he-too; Megan Gambino, "Lunch Atop a Skyscraper Photograph: The Story Behind the Famous Shot," Smithsonian, September 19, 2012, https://www.smithsonianmag.com/history/lunch-atop-a-skyscraper-photograph-the-story-behind-the-famous-shot-43931148/.

7. "Charles C. Ebbets," McGaw Graphics, accessed May 12, 2020, https://www.mcgawgraphics .com/collections/charles-c-ebbets.

8. Amy Hotz, "A Photo Finished," StarNews Online, November, 10, 2003, http://www .starnewsonline.com/news/20031110/photo-finished (interview of Tami Ebbets Hahn regarding her father's famous picture).

9. Marvel Characters, Inc. v. Kirby, 726 F.3d 119, 125–26 (2d Cir. 2013) (finding Kirby's work was for-hire and that his employer Marvel held the interest in the original copyright).

10. Brookes Barnes, "Marvel Settles with Family of Comic Book Artist," New York Times, September 27, 2014, B5 (after a lengthy legal dispute, parties came to a confidential settlement to avoid a Supreme Court decision).

11. "Charles Clyde Ebbets," Wikipedia, accessed January 29, 2020, https://en.wikipedia.org /wiki/Charles_Clyde_Ebbets.

12. Goodis v. United Artists TV, 425 F.2d 397 (S.D.N.Y. 1968) (where a magazine purchased the right of first publication and the author had no intention to donate the work, copyright notice preserved the author's rights).

13. David Nimmer, Nimmer on Copyright § 26 (1985) (single notice of a collective work suffices to include the works within).

14. "First Copyright Renewals for Periodicals," Online Books Page, accessed January 29, 2020, http://onlinebooks.library.upenn.edu/cce/firstperiod.html#N (inventory of periodicals and their first copyright renewals, filed between 1950 and 1977).

15. Chase v. Warner Bros. Entm't, 247 F. Supp. 3d 421 (S.D.N.Y. 2017).

16. "Copyright Registrations for 1960," Online Books Page, accessed January 29, 2020, http:// onlinebooks.library.upenn.edu/cce/1960r.html (tables of contents and summaries for copyright registrations for 1960).

17. "Copyright Registrations for 1961," Online Books Page, accessed January 29, 2020, http:// onlinebooks.library.upenn.edu/cce/1961r.html (tables of contents and summaries for copyright registrations for 1961).

18. Fact checking in pre-1976 records can be done only in the Copyright Office.

19. Richard Kluger, The Paper: Life and Death of the New York Herald Tribune (New York: Knopf, 1986).

20. "Partners in Herald Tribune Acquire Whitcom's Stake," New York Times, April 27, 1991, https://www.nytimes.com/1991/04/27/business/partners-in-herald-tribune-acquire-whitcom-s-stake .html (Herald purchased for an undisclosed price by the New York Times and Washington Post).

21. I ran a records check and found no filing with the words "herald tribune."

22. "New York Tribune," Wikipedia, accessed January 29, 2020, https://en.wikipedia.org/ wiki/New-York_Tribune (original articles from the New York Herald Tribune are kept at the Center for American History at University of Texas at Austin).

23. "The Online Books Page," Online Books Page, accessed January 29, 2020, http:// onlinebooks.library.upenn.edu/cce/ (works of art; reproductions of works of art; scientific and technical drawings; photographic works; prints and pictorial illustrations for 1968–73).

24. US Copyright Office, Orphan Works and Mass Digitization: A Report of the Register of Copyrights (Washington, DC: US Copyright Office, 2015) (legislation proposed to allow use of

works after prospective user has conducted a "diligent search" but failed to locate the original work).

25. "Copyright: Orphan Works," Information Site for Central Government, May 12, 2015, https://www.gov.uk/guidance/copyright-orphan-works (UK user website with instructions for copying a creative work when the original holder cannot be found).

Chapter Two

1. Andy Hermann, "Smug Turd of a Pop Song 'Blurred Lines' Has Now Ruined the Music Industry," Village Voice, March 13, 2015, https://www.villagevoice.com/author/andyhermann.

2. Robin Thicke, "Blurred Lines," YouTube, May 30, 2013, https://www.youtube.com/watch?v=yyDUC1LUXSU.

3. Marvin Gaye, "Got to Give It Up," YouTube, May 22, 2012, https://www.youtube.com/watch?v=Ayyy-o3ITDg.

4. Williams v. Gaye, 885 F.3d 1150 (9th Cir. 2018) (jury award to Gaye estate of 50 percent of running royalty was appropriate).

5. Arnstein v. Porter, 154 F.2d 464, 473 (2d Cir. 1946).

6. Axis of Awesome, "4 Chord Song (With Song Titles)," YouTube, December 10, 2009, https://www.youtube.com/watch?v=5pidokakU4I (comedy band performs mash-up of songs that contain the same four base chords).

7. Kara Brown, "A Brief History of Pop Stars Borrowing from Other Artists," Muse, May 16, 2016, https://themuse.jezebel.com/beyonce-lady-gaga-drake-a-brief-history-of-pop-star-1776813614; "27 Pop Song You Didn't Know Were Inspired by Classical Pieces," Classic fM, accessed January 29, 2020, http://www.classicfm.com/discover-music/periods-genres/modern/classical-music-pop-songs/ (27 pop songs that have same base chords).

8. Robert Raines, Composition in the Digital World: Conversations with the 21st Century (Oxford: Oxford University Press, 2015); Georg Predota, "Good Composers Borrow, Great Ones Steal!," Interlude, July 24, 2016, http://www.interlude.hk/front/good-composers-borrow-great-ones-steal.

9. Honey Meconi, Early Musical Borrowing (London: Routledge, 2015); Sienna Wood, "Musical Borrowing and Appropriation," Music Crash Courses, accessed May 13, 2020, http://www.musiccrashcourses.com/lessons/borrowing.html (essay on genres borrowing familiar melodies or base chords and when that changes into hostile appropriation).

10. Elvis Costello, Unfaithful Music and Disappearing Ink (New York: Penguin Random House, 2015), 33.

11. "Stairway to Heaven vs Taurus Guitar Examination Led Zeppelin vs Spirit," YouTube, November 20, 2014, https://www.youtube.com/watch?v=PCEg9gMJakU.

12. Skidmore v. Led Zeppelin, Nos. 16-56057, 16-56287, 2018 U.S. App. LEXIS 27680 (9th Cir. Sept. 28, 2018); Skidmore v. Led Zeppelin, No. CV 15-3462, 2016 U.S. Dist. LEXIS 51006, 9 (C.D. Cal. Apr. 8, 2016) (expert comparison between "Stairway to Heaven" and Taurus).

13. Jon Blistein, "A New Led Zeppelin Court Win over 'Stairway to Heaven' Just Upended a Copyright Precedent," Rolling Stone, March 9, 2020, https://www.rollingstone.com/music/music-news/led-zeppelin-stairway-to-heaven-copyright-infringement-ruling-appeal-964530/.

14. David Meltzer, Quotation and Cultural Meaning in 20th Century Music (Cambridge:

Cambridge University Press, 2003); "Musical Quotation," Wikipedia, accessed January 29, 2020, https://en.wikipedia.org/wiki/Musical_quotation ("Musical quotation is the practice of directly quoting another work in a new composition.").

15.   Lionel A. F. Bently & Tanya Aplin, "Whatever Became of Global Mandatory Fair Use? A Case Study in Dysfunctional Pluralism," University of Cambridge Faculty of Law Research Papers, No. 24/3018 (2018).

16.   Nelson-Salabes v. Morningside Dev., 284 F.3d 505 (4th Cir. 2002).

17.   Pamela Samuelson, "Contu Revisited: The Case Against Copyright Protection for Computer Programs in Machine Readable Form," 1984 Duke L.J. 663.

18.   Computer Assocs. v. Altai, 982 F.2d 693, 710–11 (2d Cir. 1992).

19.   Swirsky v. Carey, 376 F.3d 841, 853 (9th Cir. 2004) (there is no copyright protection if there is no originality in the similar work).

Chapter Three

1.   Larry Rohter, "A Copyright Victory, 35 Years Later," New York Times, September 10, 2013, C1; Eriq Gardner, "Village People Songwriter Victor Willis Wins Case over Termination of 'Y.M.C.A.' Rights," Hollywood Reporter, May 8, 2012, https://www.hollywoodreporter.com/thresq/village-people-ymca-lawsuit-victor-willis-321576 (one of the three songwriters of "Y.M.C.A." was granted termination rights to his shares, which could cause a revenue jump and other artists seeking similar termination).

2.   Sharon LaFraniere, "In the Jungle, the Unjust Jungle, a Small Victory," New York Times, March 22, 2006, https://www.nytimes.com/2006/03/22/world/africa/in-the-jungle-the-unjust-jungle-a-small-victory.html.

3.   Rian Malan, "In the Jungle: Inside the Long, Hidden, Genealogy of 'The Lion Sleeps Tonight,'" Rolling Stone, May 14, 2000, https://www.rollingstone.com/music/music-features/in-the-jungle-inside-the-long-hidden-genealogy-of-the-lion-sleeps-tonight-108274/ (American musicians made millions off a Zulu tribesman's song, and he saw almost no revenue).

4.   "All Time Box Office," Box Office Mojo, accessed January 29, 2020, https://www.boxofficemojo.com/alltime/ (listing the highest grossing box office movies, The Lion King at highest overall rated "G").

5.   Random House v. Rosetta Books, 150 F. Supp. 2d 613, 620 (S.D.N.Y. 2001) ("Random House contends that the phrase 'in book form' means to faithfully reproduce the author's text in its complete form as a reading experience and that, since ebooks concededly contain the complete text of the work, Rosetta cannot also possess those rights.").

6.   Random House, 150 F. Supp. 2d at 621–23.

7.   Martin Kretschmer, "Copyright Term Reversion and the 'Use It or Lose It' Principle," International Journal of Music Business Research 1, no. 1 (2012): 24.

8.   Michael D. Smith, Rahul Telang, and Yi Zhang, "Analysis of the Potential Market for Out-of-Print eBooks" (Heinz College School of Information Systems and Management Carnegie Mellon Univ., 2012).

9.   Chloe Chaplain, "Burberry Burned $37 Million Worth of Goods to Stop Them Being Stolen or Sold Cheaply," Business Insider International, July 19, 2018, https://www.businessinsider.de/

burberry-burned-37-million-of-goods-to-protect-its-brand-2018-7?r=US&IR=T.

10. Edwin McDowell, "Clavell: King of Commercial Fiction?," New York Times, November 17, 1986, https://www.nytimes.com/1986/11/17/books/clavell-king-of-commercial-fiction.html (detailing James Clavell's deal with publishers).

11. John B. Thompson, Merchants of Culture (Cambridge: Polity Press, 2011); "E-Book," Wikipedia, accessed January 29, 2020, https://en.wikipedia.org/wiki/E-book#cite_note-30 (the history of the e-book).

12. Associated Press, "Humphrey Lyttelton, 86, Host of a BBC Radio Game Show," New York Times, April 28, 2008, B7 (obituary).

Chapter Four

1. Jeremy Smith, "10 Movies Based on Classic Books That Went Horribly Wrong," Thrillist Entertainment, August 9, 2017, https://www.thrillist.com/entertainment/nation/worst-movies -based-on-books.

2. Tasha Espinoza, "Metacritic's Best and Worst Movies Based on Novels," Metacritic, December 15, 2009, https://www.metacritic.com/feature/best-and-worst-movies-based-on-novels.

3. Fidel Martinez, "The 10 Worst Movies Based on Children's Books," Yardbarker, February 6, 2018, https://www.yardbarker.com/entertainment/articles/the_10_worst_movies_based_on _childrens_books/s1__25637669#slide_1.

4. Palko Karasz, "An Opera Troup Defends a Mostly White 'Porgy,'" New York Times, February 2, 2018, C6.

5. Louisa Schaefer, "White Cast of 'Porgy and Bess' Opera in Hungary provokes Debate on Artistic Freedom," posted January 2, 2018, on DW.com, https://www.dw.com/en/white-cast-of -porgy-and-bess-opera-in-hungary-provokes-debate-on-artistic-freedom/a-42398353.

6. Alan Dessen, Elizabethan Stage Conventions and Modern Interpretations (Cambridge: Cambridge University Press, 1984), 8–11 (describing how modern interpretations of Shakespeare include staging that detracts rather than adds meaning); David Cote, "Most Stagings of Shakespeare Don't Go Far Enough," Theatre Blog, Guardian, January 19, 2010, https://www.theguardian .com/stage/theatreblog/2010/jan/19/shakespeare-modern-staging (asserting current staging of Shakespeare plays is too conceptual and does not capture the true essence of the playwright).

7. Ben Brantley, "Something Wicked This Way Comes," review of Macbeth, by William Shakespeare, directed by Rupert Goold, Brooklyn Academy of Music—Harvey Theater, Brooklyn, New York Times, February 15, 2008 (director "clearly thought through his conceit of the play as a portrait of a totalitarian tyrant and the paranoiac world he engenders").

8. Andrew Nodell, "Nude, All-Male Production of 'Hamlet' Aims to Promote Body Positivity," Women's Wear Daily, August 7, 2017, http://wwd.com/eye/lifestyle/nude-all-male-production- hamlet-body-positivity-10957498/ (director "felt the plot of 'Hamlet' was the perfect vehicle to further the conversation on body awareness," with nudity "advanc[ing] themes in the show that come up over and over again").

9. Justin Hughes, "'Recoding' Intellectual Property and Overlooked Audience Interests," Texas Law Review 77 (1999): 923.

10. Ty Inc. v. Perryman, 306 F.2d 509, 511 (7th Cir. 2002).

11. V Secret Catalogue v. Moseley, 605 F.3d 382, 388 (6th Cir. 2010).

12. Pfizer Inc. v. Sachs, 652 F. Supp. 2d 512, 525 (S.D.N.Y. 2009) (to prevail on a claim of trademark dilution, the plaintiff must show the mark is famous and that use is likely to cause dilution by tarnishment).

13. Kraft Foods Holding, Inc. v. Helm, 205 F. Supp. 2d 942, 949–50 (N.D. Ill. 2002) (slight variations in spelling and pronunciation are often insufficient to inform buyers of a difference between products).

14. Mattel, Inc. v. Internet Dimensions Inc., 55 U.S.P.Q.2d (BNA) 1620, 1627 (S.D.N.Y. 2000).

15. Polo Ralph Lauren L.P. v. Schuman, 46 U.S.P.Q.2d (BNA) 1046, 1048 (S.D. Tex. 1998) (manufacturer argued that use of the logo in an adult entertainment business violated trademark law).

16. Toys "R" Us, Inc. v. Akkaoui, No. C 96-3381 CW, 1996 WL 772709 (N.D. Cal. Oct. 29, 1996) (pornographic website called adultsrus.com tarnished the retailer's trademark).

17. Hasbro, Inc. v. Internet Entm't Grp., No. C96-130WD, 1996 WL 84853, at *1 (W.D. Wash. Feb. 9, 1996) (pornographic website called candyland.com tarnished the board game's trademark).

18. Pillsbury Co. v. Milky Way Prods., Inc., 215 U.S.P.Q. (BNA) 124, 135 (N.D. Ga. 1981) (Milky Way's use of Pillsbury's copyrighted product could injure the distinctive quality of Pillsbury's business).

19. Dallas Cowboys Cheerleaders, Inc. v. Pussycat Cinema, Ltd., 467 F. Supp. 366, 377 (S.D.N.Y. 1979) (pornographic depiction of the Dallas Cowboys cheerleaders would tarnish the trademark).

20. William Landes and Richard A. Posner, The Economic Structure of Intellectual Property Law (Cambridge, MA: Harvard University Press, 2003), 225.

21. Campbell v. Acuff-Rose Music, Inc., 510 U.S. 569 (1994) (a parody song's commercial character was one element that should be weighed in fair use inquiry).

22. Campbell, 510 U.S. at 595 (app. B).

23. Mattel, Inc. v. MCA Records, 296 F.3d 894 (9th Cir. 2002) (song "Barbie Girl" did not tarnish the Barbie brand); Mattel Inc. v. Jcomm, Inc., 1998 U.S. Dist. LEXIS 16195 (S.D.N.Y. Sept. 10, 1998) (adult entertainment website's use of the Barbie trademark diluted the brand).

24. Dr. Seuss Enters., LP v. Penguin Books USA, Inc., 109 F.3d 1394 (9th Cir. 1997).

25. Christopher Buccafusco and Paul J. Heald, "Do Bad Things Happen When Works Enter the Public Domain? Empirical Tests of Copyright Term Extension," 28 Berkeley Technology Law Journal 28 (2013): 14 (quoting Arthur Miller's concern that without perpetual ownership, nothing will stop inappropriate uses of public domain works).

26. Buccafusco and Heald, "Do Bad Things Happen?"

Chapter Five

1. Directive 2001/29, of the European Parliament and of the Council of 22 May 2001 on the Harmonisation of Certain Aspects of Copyright and Related Rights in the Information Society 2001/29/EC, 2001 O.J. (L 167) 10, 19.

2. Deckmyn v. Vandersteen [2014] All ER (D) 30 (Eng.) (laying out foundation for what constitutes a parody that does not violate copyright laws under English law); Dan Smith, "A New Law State of Mind—UK Parody Exception to Copyright Infringement Comes into Force—1 October," Gowling WLG (blog), October 2, 2014, https://gowlingwlg.com/en/insights-resources

/articles/2014/a-new-law-state-of-mind-uk-parody-exception-to-c.

3. Kris Erickson, Martin Kretschmer, and Dinusha Mendis, "Copyright and the Economic Effects of Parody: An Empirical Study of Music Videos on the YouTube Platform and an Assessment of the Regulatory Options," January 2013, https://assets.publishing.service.gov.uk/government /uploads/system/uploads/attachment_data/file/309903/ipresearch-parody-report3-150313.pdf.

4. Erickson, Kretschmer, and Mendis, "Copyright and the Economic Effects of Parody," 12.

5. Key of Awesome, "Adele—Hello PARODY! Key of Awesome #103," YouTube, November 21, 2015, https://www.youtube.com/watch?v=emG3YhU9Efg.

6. Digital Medium Copyright Act of 1998, Pub. L. No. 105-304, 112 Stat. 2860.

7. Paul J. Heald, "How Notice-and-Takedown Regimes Create Markets for Music on YouTube: An Empirical Study," UMKC Law Review 83 (2014): 313.

8. "Terms of Service," YouTube, December 10, 2019, https://www.youtube.com/ static?template=terms.

9. "Lost Television Broadcast," Wikipedia, accessed January 29, 2020, https://en.wikipedia .org/wiki/Lost_television_broadcast.

10. David Roth and Jared Diamond, "Found at Last: A Tape of the First Super Bowl," Wall Street Journal, February 5, 2011, A16 ("No recording of the 1967 Packers-Chiefs game had ever been found—until this one emerged from a Pennsylvania attic").

11. "Lost Television Broadcast."

12. Library of Congress, Film Preservation Board, A Study of the Current State of American Television and Video Preservation, vol. 2, Hearing Before the Panel of the Library of Congress (1996) (statement of Edie Adams regarding the disposal of three truckloads of tapes into the harbor).

Chapter Six

1. Johannes Brahms, 3 Sacred Choruses, Op. 37 (1859).

2. Johann Sebastian Bach, Italian Concerto, 3rd movement, Sheet Music Direct, accessed January 29, 2020, https://www.sheetmusicdirect.com/se/ID_No/117889/Product.aspx.

3. "False Copyright Claims are More Common Than You Think," Public Domain Sherpa, accessed January 29, 2020, http://www.publicdomainsherpa.com/false-copyright-claims.html

4. Paul J. Heald, "Reviving the Rhetoric of the Public Interest: Choir Directors, Copy Machines, and New Arrangements of Public Domain Music," Duke Law Journal 46 (1996): 241.

5. Heald, "Reviving the Rhetoric."

6. Jason Mazzone, Copyfraud and Other Abuses of Intellectual Property Law (Stanford, CA: Stanford University Press, 2011).

7. "Roll Over Beethoven," YouTube, October 5, 2008, https://www.youtube.com/ watch?v=CxXl40S9wss.

8. Danilo Lazevic, "Balkan Beats: Introducing Folk Rap, the Hybrid Music Craze Sweeping Serbia and Beyond," Calvert Journal, May 9, 2018, https://www.calvertjournal.com/articles /show/9932/balkan-beats-folk-rap.

9. M. William Krasilovsky and Sidney Shemel, The Business of Music (7th ed. 1995), 262.

10. Uncle Sam mechanical bank, Wikipedia Commons, accessed January 29, 2020, https://commons.wikimedia.org/wiki/File:Uncle_Sam_mechanical_bank.jpg.

11. L. Batlin & Son, Inc. v. Snyder, 536 F.2d 486, 492 (2d Cir. 1976).

12. Woods v. Bourne Co., 60 F.3d 978 (2d Cir. 1995).

13. David Ewen, Popular American Composers from Revolutionary Times to the Present, a Biographical and Critical Guide (New York: H. W. Wilson, 1962).

14. Jack Burton, "The Honor Roll of Popular Songwriters," Billboard, February 24, 1951, 36.

15. Woods v. Bourne Co., 841 F. Supp. 118, 121 (S.D.N.Y. 1994).

16. Cooper v. James, 213 F. 871 (N.D. Ga. 1914) (addition of a new part to a well-known tune does not constitute original composing worthy of a new copyright).

17. Id. at 873.

18. Tempo Music v. Famous Music Corp., 838 F. Supp. 162 (S.D.N.Y. 1993).

19. Wood v. Boosey, 3 L.R.-Q.B. 223 (1868).

20. Paul J. Heald, "Payment Demands for Spurious Copyrights: Four Causes of Action," Journal of Intellectual Property Law 1 (1994): 259–92.

21. Tams-Witmark Music Library v. New Opera Co., 71 N.Y.S.2d 136 (N.Y. App. Div. 1947).

22. Restatement of Restitution (Washington, DC: American Law Institute, 1937), § 24.

23. Page Keeton et al., Prosser and Keeton on Torts, 5th ed. (Minneapolis: West, 1984), § 107, at 748.

24. Ga. Code Ann. § 51-12-5.1(b) (Michie 1993) (emphasis added); Tex. Civ. Prac. & Rem. Code Ann. § 41.003(a) (West Supp. 1994) ("Exemplary damages may be awarded only if the claimant proves that the personal injury, property damage, death, or other harm with respect to which the claimant seeks recovery of exemplary damages results from: (1) fraud; (2) malice; or (3) gross negligence.").

25. Kenneth A. Plevan and Miriam Siroky, Advertising Compliance Handbook (New York: Practising Law Institute, 1994), 289–91; see, e.g., Cal. Bus. & Prof. Code §§ 17200, 17500–17577 (West 1987 & Supp. 1990); 121 Ill. Comp. Stat. Ann. 5/261 (West 1989); N.Y. Gen. Bus. Law §§ 349–350 (McKinney 1988 & Supp. 1989).

26. In re Cliffdale, 103 F.T.C. 110, 190–96 (1984); "Federal Trade Commission Policy Statement on Deception," issued October 14, 1983, reprinted in 45 Antitrust & Trade Reg. Rptr. (BNA) 689 (1983).

27. EFS Marketing v. Russ Berrie & Co., 836 F. Supp. 128 (S.D.N.Y. 1993), vacated, 76 F.3d 487 (2d Cir. 1996).

28. Edmund Kitch and Harvey Perlman, Legal Regulation of the Competitive Process, rev. 4th ed. (Minneapolis: Foundation Press, 1991).

29. Brooks v. Midas Int'l Corp., 361 N.E.2d 815 (Ill. App. Ct. 1977).

30. Hayna v. Arby's Inc., 425 N.E.2d 1174 (Ill. App. Ct. 1981).

31. State ex rel. Guste v. Gen. Motors Corp., 370 So. 2d 477 (La. 1978) (misrepresentation concerning brand of car engine); Compact Electra Corp. v. Paul, 403 N.Y.S.2d 611 (Sup. Ct. 1977) (consistent misrepresentations concerning vacuum cleaners made in sales); Amato v. Gen. Motors Corp., 463 N.E.2d 625 (Ohio Ct. App. 1982) (misrepresentation concerning brand of car engine).

Chapter Seven

1. Intellectual Property Office, "Guide to Evidence for Policy," accessed January 29, 2020, https://assets.publishing.service.gov.uk/government/uploads/system/uploads/attachment_data /file/510985/Guide_to_evidence_for_policy.pdf.

2. Intellectual Property Office, "Creative Industries' Record Contribution to UK Economy," November 29, 2017, https://www.gov.uk/government/news/creative-industries-record-contribution -to-uk-economy.

3. Jesse Jarnow, "The Invisible Hit Parade: How Unofficial Recordings Have Flowered in the 21st Century," Wired, November 21, 2018, https://www.wired.com/story/invisible-hit-parade -live-concert-taping/.

4. Creative Commons, accessed January 29, 2020, https://creativecommons.org/.

5. Wikimedia Commons, accessed January 29, 2020, https://commons.wikimedia.org/wiki/ Main_Page (collection of usable media files that anyone can use or contribute to).

6. Rose Eveleth, "How Much is Wikipedia Worth?", Smithsonian, October 7, 2013, https:// www.smithsonianmag.com/smart-news/how-much-is-wikipedia-worth-704865/.

7. Brigit Bennet, The Damnation of Harold Frederic: His Lives and Works (Syracuse: Syracuse University Press, 1997).

8. Gary Marx, "Survivors See Little Sense Behind the Terror," Chicago Tribune, April 5, 1996, https://www.chicagotribune.com/news/ct-xpm-1996-04-05-9604050280-story.html.

9. It may well be that Van Vechten's photos are in the public domain due to failure to renew the copyright.

10. "How to Increase Traffic to Your Website with the Help of Images," Koozai (blog), July 12, 2013, https://www.koozai.com/blog/content-marketing-seo/increase-traffic-with-images/.

11. "List of Premature Obituaries," accessed January 29, 2020, https://en.wikipedia.org/wiki/ List_of_premature_obituaries (Rudyard Kipling erroneously pronounced dead).

12. "File: Rudyard Kipling.jpg," accessed January 29, 2020, https://commons.wikimedia. org/wiki/File:Rudyard_Kipling.jpg.

13. Buccafusco and Heald, "Do Bad Things Happen?," 5.

14. Michale Hiltzik, "Getty Images Will Bill You Thousands to Use a Photo That Belongs to the Public. Is That Legal?" L.A. Times, August 2, 2016, http://www.latimes.com/business/hiltzik/ la-fi-hiltzik-getty-photos-20160801-snap-story.html.

15. Complaint, Highsmith v. Getty Images, Inc., No. 16 Civ. 5924 (S.D.N.Y. July 25, 2016).

16. Kris Erickson, Felix Rodriguez Perez, and Jesus Rodriguez Perez, "What Is the Commons Worth? Estimating the Value of Wikimedia Imagery by Observing Downstream Use" (paper, OpenSym '18: The 14th International Symposium on Open Collaboration, Paris, August 22–24, 2018), https://papers.ssrn.com/sol3/papers.cfm?abstract_id=3206188.

17. Erickson, Perez, and Perez, "What Is the Commons Worth?"

18. Gwen Davis, Touching, accessed January 29, 2020, https://www.amazon.com/ Touching-Gwen-Davis-ebook/dp/B00757TVJC/ref=sr_1_1?ie=UTF8&qid=1524140836&sr=8 -1&keywords=touching+gwen+davis (blurb describing book).

19. Bindrim v. Mitchell, 155 Cal. Rptr. 29 (Cal. Ct. App. 1979).

20. I counted 96 billion page views from August 2017 to August 2018. "Siteviews Analysis,"

Wikimedia Toolforge, accessed January 29, 2020, https://tools.wmflabs.org/siteviews/?platform=all -access&source=pageviews&agent=user&start=2017-08-06&end=2018-08-26&sites=en.wikipedia.org.

21. Paul J. Heald, Kristopher Erickson, and Martin Kretschmer, "The Valuation of Public Domain Works: A Case Study of Public Domain Images on Wikipedia," Harvard Journal of Law and Technology 29 (2015): 1.

22. Heald, Erickson, and Kretschmer, "Valuation of Public Domain Works," 28.

Chapter Eight

1. Joel Waldfogel, Digital Renaissance (Princeton, NJ: Princeton University Press, 2018), 103.

2. Glynn Lunney, Copyright's Excess: Money and Music in the US Recording Industry (Cambridge: University Printing House, 2018), 143.

3. Kerry Segrave, Payola in the Music Industry: A History, 1880–1991 (Jefferson, NC: McFarland, 1994).

4. Waldrogel, Digital Renaissance, 20.

5. Waldfogel, Digital Renaissance, 8–9, "Bieber was discovered in 2008 by Scooter Braun, who happened to come across Bieber's videos on YouTube and later became his manager. Braun arranged for him to meet with Usher in Atlanta, Georgia, and Bieber was soon signed to Raymond Braun Media Group (RBMG), a joint venture between Braun and Usher, and then to a recording contract with Island Records offered by L. A. Reid. His debut single, "One Time," released worldwide in 2009, peaked in the top ten in Canada and charted in the top thirty in several international markets. His debut release, My World, followed on November 17, 2009, and was eventually certified platinum in the US. He became the first artist to have seven songs from a debut album chart on the Billboard Hot 100."

6. Lunney, Copyright's Excess.

7. "List of Most Expensive Films," Wikipedia, accessed January 29, 2020, https://en.wikipedia.org/wiki/List_of_most_expensive_films.

8. Stop On-Line Piracy Act, H.R. 3261, 112th Cong. (2011).

9. Feist, Inc. v. Rural Tel. Serv., 499 U.S. 340, 349–50 (1991).

10. The Scope of Copyright Protection: Hearing before the Subcomm. on Courts, Intellectual Property, and the Internet of the H. Comm. on the Judiciary, 113th Cong. (2014), https://www.govinfo.gov/content/pkg/CHRG-113hhrg86344/html/CHRG-113hhrg86344.htm (testimony of Glynn S. Lunney Jr., McGlinchey Stafford Professor of Law, Tulane University Law School).

Chapter Nine

1. Kirtsaeng v. John Wiley & Sons, Inc., 568 U.S. 519 (2013).

2. Saira Stewart, "HIV Treatment Now Reaching More Than 6 Million People in the Sub-Saharan Africa," UNAIDS Geneva, July 6, 2012, http://www.unaids.org/en/resources/presscentre/pressreleaseandstatementarchive/2012/july/20120706prafricatreatment.

3. "Brands and Companies," Swatch Group, accessed January 29, 2020, http://www.swatchgroup.com/brands_and_companies/distribution.

4. Agreement on Trade-Related Aspects of Intellectual Property Rights, April 15, 1994, Marrakesh Agreement Establishing the Word Trade Organization, art. 4, U.N.T.S. 299 (1994).

5. John Wiley & Sons, Inc. v. Kirtsaeng, 654 F.3d 210 (2d Cir. 2010).

6. Kirtsaeng, 568 U.S. at 542.

7. Kirtsaeng, 568 U.S. at 542.

Chapter Ten

1. The RIAA has total industry sales data going back until 1973, but it does not publish how many copies of each song were sold during that era.

2. William Landes and Richard Posner, "Indefinitely Renewable Copyright," University of Chicago Law Review 70 (2003): 471.

3. "Surprising Origins of 100-Year-Old Danny Boy," CBS News, December 31, 2013, https://www.cbsnews.com/news/surprising-origins-of-100-year-old-danny-boy/.

4. Julius Mattfeld, Variety Music Cavalcade, 1620–1969, 3rd ed. (Englewood Cliffs, NJ: Prentice-Hall, 1971).

5. Carl Orff, Carmina Burana: Choral Score (Mainz: Schott Musik, 2007).

6. Justin Hughes, "'Recoding' Intellectual Property and Overlooked Audience Interests," Texas Law Review 77 (1999): 923, 930.

7. David Graham, "Sigh of the Tiger," Atlantic, September 10, 2015, https://www.theatlantic.com/politics/archive/2015/09/musicians-politics-anger/404629/. (R.E.M. outraged that Donald Trump used their song in campaign ad without permission and when they do not support him as a candidate.)

Chapter Eleven

1. Buccafusco and Heald, "Do Bad Things Happen?," 7.

2. Buccafusco and Heald, "Do Bad Things Happen?," 7.

3. Buccafusco and Heald, "Do Bad Things Happen?," 7.

4. Timothy Lee, "15 Years Ago, Congress Kept Mickey Mouse Out of the Public Domain. Will They Do It Again?," Washington Post, October 25, 2013, https://www.washingtonpost.com/news/the-switch/wp/2013/10/25/15-years-ago-congress-kept-mickey-mouse-out-of-the-public-domain-will-they-do-it-again/?utm_term=.a92b6f3b2f85.

5. Eldred v. Ashcroft, 537 U.S. 186 (2003).

6. District of Columbia v. Heller, 554 U.S. 570 (2008).

7. "Anthony (Fat Tony) Salerno, 80, a Top Crime Boss, Dies in Prison," New York Times, July 29, 1992, https://www.nytimes.com/1992/07/29/us/anthony-fat-tony-salerno-80-a-top-crime-boss-dies-in-prison.html.

8. Paul J. Heald and Suzanna Sherry, "Implied Limits on the Legislative Power: The Intellectual Property Clause as an Absolute Constraint on Congress," University of Illinois Law Review 2000:1119, 1170.

9. Darcy v. Allein (1602), 74 Eng. Rep. 1131.

10. Heald and Sherry, "Implied Limits," 1171.

11. Graham v. John Deere Co., 383 U.S. 1 (1966).

12. "Rational Basis Review," Black's Law Dictionary, 10th ed. (Minneapolis: West, 2014).

13. Robert C. Farrell, "Successful Rational Basis Claims in the Supreme Court From the

1971 Term Through Romer v. Evans," Indiana Law Review 32 (1999): 357, 372.

14. Weinberger v. Wiesenfeld, 420 U.S. 636 (1975).

15. Stanton v. Stanton, 421 U.S. 7 (1975).

16. Marbury v. Madison, 5 U.S. 137 (1803).

17. Robert Brauneis, "A Brief Illustrated Chronicle of Copyright Term Extension," George Washington School of Law Faculty Commons, 2015, https://scholarship.law.gwu.edu/cgi/viewcontent.cgi?article=2512&context=faculty_publications.

18. Laurence Tribe, "Taking Text and Structure Seriously: Reflections on Free-Form Method in Constitutional Interpretation," Harvard Law Review 108 (1995): 799.

19. INS v. Chadha, 462 U.S. 919 (1983).

20. Youngstown Sheet & Tube Co. v. Sawyer, 343 U.S. 579 (1952).

21. Peter Spiro, "Treaties, Executive Agreement, and Constitutional Method," Texas Law Review 79 (2001): 961.

22. 15 U.S.C. §§ 101–103 (2018).

23. Reid v. Covert, 354 U.S. 1, 16 (1957).

24. Unknown, December 3, 2014, comment on St. Estephe, "Clarice B. Covert, Axe Murderess – 1953," Unknown Misandry (blog), July 20, 2011, http://unknownmisandry.blogspot.com/2011/07/clarice-b-covert-axe-murderess-1953.html.

25. Paul J. Heald, "Property Rights and the Efficient Exploitation of Copyrighted Works: An Empirical Analysis of Public Domain and Copyrighted Fiction Bestsellers," Minnesota Law Review 92, no. 4 (2008): 1051.

Conclusion

1. The pricing data from Canada, the UK, and South Africa has not yet been published but can be obtained from the author.

INDEX

9 781503 613959